# How to Function in this Economy According to Heaven's Economy

# What Ministers Are Saying

"Gerald's ministry on faith and finances would be a blessing to any church....he really blessed us at Lakewood Church....one of my favorite preachers....a pastor at large...."—**Pastors John & Dodie Osteen, Lakewood Church, Houston, TX**

"Our people were impressed by the simplicity of your answers to every question....one of the best sermons I've ever heard."—**Pastor Happy Caldwell, Agape Ministries, President of ICFM Fellowship U.S.A., Little Rock, AR**

"Gerald has the ability to draw out the scriptures and make the Christian walk come alive....the integrity and sincerity of this man seems to transform his audience....a powerful anointing."—**Pastor Gary Greenwald, Eagle's Nest, Santa Ana, CA**

"Gerald's insight is unique and fresh....thoroughly understands the operation of the local church...."—**Pastor Tom Peters, Trinity A/G, Lake Worth, FL**

"It is very evident that his years of experience and deep commitment to God's Word have made Gerald one of the top Bible teachers in the land today."—**Pastor Keith Johnson, Christian Center Ministries, President of Ministries Fellowship, Saskatoon, Canada**

"We have signs following his ministry weeks after he has gone....accuracy and of reputable character."—**Dr. Mark Barclay, Pastor of Living Word Outreach, Midland, MI**

"Preaching that anyone can relate to....a positive preacher."—**Evelyn Roberts, Author and Wife of Oral Roberts, President of ORU, Tulsa, OK**

# How to Function
# in this Economy
# According to
# Heaven's Economy

Dr. Gerald W. Davis

With a foreword by Dr. Reginald Klimionok

FAME Publishing, Incorporated
Coppell, Texas

FAME Publishing, Incorporated
820 S. MacArthur Blvd., Suite 105-220
Coppell, Texas 75019-5574

99 98 97 96 95 94     5 4 3 2 1

ISBN 1-880563-08-8

# Dedication

I dedicate this book to my two especially fine sons, Jerry and Tommy; also to their lovely wives, Melinda and Debbie; and to my grandchildren, Tiffany and Andrea (twin girls), Crystal, Lisa, Justin (my only grandson), and Victoria.

A father could not be more fulfilled and proud of his sons and their dedication to God than this father. Jerry travels the world over in missionary evangelism, and Tommy owns automobile businesses and strongly supports the Gospel ministry.

David said in Psalm 127:3, 5 "Children are an heritage of the Lord....Happy is the man that hath his quiver full...." This certainly describes the life I have. I am a happy man.

# Contents

# Foreword

Dr. Gerald Davis is uniquely gifted to give the church of Jesus Christ an understanding of God's financial plan for His People.

In these pages you will find clear principles that are strongly backed by the Word of God and Scriptural examples. This is a "handbook" on how God views finances and one that every Christian home should have. It gives solutions to the problems of this modern hour, when many Christians find themselves struggling with heavy financial pressures and burdens. I believe it is a gold mine for preachers who are looking for answers that they can share with their congregations on God's provisions and their own response in giving.

This book, *How to Function in this Economy According to Heaven's Economy*, comes with a fresh, balanced outlook on the subject. It has been boldly tackled by Dr. Davis with maturity that comes from his rich Christian heritage coupled with many years of ministry and study of the Word of God.

It has been my pleasure to have Dr. Davis minister for me on several occasions at Evangelistic Temple. He presents a very powerful message; and each time our congregation has been blessed, and many lives have been transformed in these financial areas through receiving the Truth according to "Heaven's Economy."

Dr. Reginald Klimionok
Senior Pastor of Evangelistic Temple, Houston, Texas
International Teacher and Author

# Preface

It was November of 1979. Thelma, my wife, and I were returning from our first overseas missionary journey together. The drone from the engines of the Korean jet airliner was helping my weary body to sleep. Not only was I tired, but I was running a low-grade fever. However, as I started to awaken, my mind drifted back over the past 30 days.

With our own eyes, Thelma and I had seen it all in India and Sri Lanka. We had seen both the physical and spiritual hunger of the people in those countries. We had preached to thousands who had never heard the Gospel. Untold numbers denounced their gods to accept Jesus Christ as their Savior. Not only this, but multitudes were miraculously healed and delivered from demon possession. So, why was I experiencing such a strange, unexplainable feeling?

After traveling for over one month, we finally arrived home. Once again I was in my own bed and eating good food. Could this be the reason that I was feeling strangely? As I mused, I had in my spirit an unexplainable desire to preach in the U.S. Thelma and I had often joked about having a church on every other corner, so the Gospel could be plentifully proclaimed.

I asked, "God, what are You saying to me? What are You asking me?"

The message came through very clearly. God gave me a revelation as to what my part was to be. Through this missionary journey, God birthed our ministry. Both in India and Sri Lanka, Thelma and I had seen many wonderful things happen. Yet it was as if we had just splashed a drop of water on a forest fire. We knew what needed to be accomplished, but the cost would be enormous. Remember, Jesus said:

> ...The harvest truly is plenteous, but the labourers are few;
>
> Pray ye therefore the Lord of the harvest, that he will send forth labourers into his harvest.
>
> Matthew 9:37-38

It was after this missionary trip that God gave me a glimpse of the ministry He was calling me to launch. He imparted to me a very powerful revelation concerning the controversial subject of prosperity, and that was to be the thrust of my ministry.

So, after 24 years of pastoring and evangelizing, I started teaching and preaching messages concerning the subject of prosperity throughout the U.S. and abroad. Now, after almost 15 years of teaching this message, God continues to reveal His Truth to me. The prosperity of His children is very dear to Him.

Now I am sharing this material as a "textbook" and a "teaching manual." This I am doing so it may be used to help reach the unsaved multitudes before the return of our Lord and Savior, Jesus Christ.

# Acknowledgments

Thanks to
my brother and sister-in-law, David and Janet Waters,
and my niece, Charlyn Taylor,
for helping in the preparation of this manuscript.

Thanks to
my sister-in-law, Dolly Davis,
for designing this book cover,
and for her expert help and assistance.

Thanks to
Mark Pendergrass
for creating the cover art work.

A special thanks to Thelma,
my wife since 1954,
for faithfully walking by my side, step by step,
and for her devoted help in coordinating this book.

# Introduction

The Apostle Paul admonishes us concerning the salvation of the multitudes of unsaved people throughout the world.

> **For whosoever shall call upon the name of the Lord shall be saved.**
>
> **How then shall they call on him in whom they have not believed? and how shall they believe in him of whom they have not heard? and how shall they hear without a preacher?**
> **Romans 10:13-14**

Certain questions involving this Scripture come into my mind. *How can preachers be sent without money? How can we (as believers) send them if we do not have the money?*

Obviously, the ungodly are not going to voluntarily sponsor preachers. Then who will?

**Believers are the only ones who care!**

But if we pray only to have enough funds for our own personal needs, then we will not have the millions of dollars necessary to channel into reaching the masses with the Gospel.

**So, how can we fulfill the Great Commission?**

The Great Commission is a commandment, not a suggestion:

> Go ye therefore, and teach all nations, baptizing them in the name of the Father, and of the Son, and of the Holy Ghost:
>
> Teaching them to observe all things whatsoever I have commanded you: and, lo, I am with you alway, even unto the end of the world.
>
> **Matthew 28:19-20**

This promise of the Father is to them that "go" or "send." In other words, the same promise is for those who go out into the mission field (both local and abroad) and for those who send others.

It is because of this issue that I write this book. I will deal with the many questions God has helped me to resolve satisfactorily.

My files contain many letters from individuals and ministries with whom I have shared these truths. People are writing of their increase both in understanding and in finances.

My prayer is that (after you study this book) you, too, will have gained more knowledge and answers to your questions concerning this subject.

Some of the revelations I share may be new to you. Also, they may challenge some of your traditional beliefs. Yet, every thought is within the framework of the question posed: *How can they go except they be sent?* I pray that what develops in your spirit is a fresh revelation from God.

At present, Christianity is losing ground in the population growth of the world.

**Something must change!** Will you (as I have) **accept the challenge?**

If you keep on doing what you have always done, you will always have what you have always had.

# 1

# The Father's Need

Did you know that God has needs, too? *His* dreams are closely tied with *your* needs—your personal prayer requests this very moment. In fact, when you help God to satisfy *His* needs, you will begin to see *your* dreams come true.

However, before you can understand God's needs, you must know His nature. Now consider with me the nature of God our Father. Jesus helped us to know His Father by comparing *our* nature with *God's* nature. He asked the disciples this question:

> **If ye then, being evil, know how to give good gifts unto your children,** *how much more* **shall our Father which is in heaven** *give good things* **to His Children?**
> **Matthew 7:11, paraphrased**

Jesus also taught that "...It is more blessed to give than to receive" (Acts 20:35). The Bible frequently refers to God giving of Himself to us. **Giving is the nature of God.**

- "For God so loved...that He **gave...**" (John 3:16).
- "...The Son of man came **not** to be ministered unto,

3

but **to minister..."** (Matthew 20:28).

- "...Go ye and learn what that meaneth, I will have mercy, and not sacrifice..." (Matthew 9:13). Jesus was explaining that He came **to show mercy**—to give—not to receive your sacrifice.

God teaches us that all our giving is designed for *our* advantage. God does not need material things. **He has it all.** His desire is to **give it to us.** God's nature is to give. *He has a need to give.*

## My Discovery

As I was praying one day, I began to intercede about the problems of some people in the church I pastored. I was laying these needs out one by one before God when the thought came to me, "I wonder if *God* ever has any needs?"

Instantly, in my spirit I heard God answer, "Yes I do! Go find out what they are and tell it everywhere you go."

That was over 15 years ago, but I have never forgotten what the Lord showed me in Scripture that day at my office.

Reflect with me now as I share what God gave me that day. It begins with the story of creation. In chapter one of Genesis, God created the universe and everything in it. Then on the sixth and last day of creation, "...God said, Let us make man in our image, after our likeness..." (Genesis 1:26).

**Now notice how God's next statement revealed His purpose for making man,** *"And let them have...."* As soon as God created man, He blessed him and urged, "...Be fruitful, and multiply...and have dominion over the fish of the sea, and over the fowl of the air, and over every living thing that moveth upon the earth" (Genesis 1:28).

4

Then in verse 29, God leaned back, breathed deeply, and sighed as He said, "...Behold, **I have given**...." Again in verse 30 He said, "**...I have given**...." After God had given creation to man He was satisfied. "And God saw every thing that he had made, and behold, it was very good" (Genesis 1:31).

God's need was fulfilled.

He wanted to have someone of His own likeness to whom He could give good gifts. That is why God created you and me to be His children—so He could give His best gifts to us!

In fact, we are so close to the likeness of God that we will judge the angels (I Corinthians 6:3)! It did not satisfy God to give His riches to angels. He needed children to whom He could give His riches. *We* are the "heirs of God" (Romans 8:17).

## Satan's Displeasure

Remember what happened next. Satan, who hates God, could not stand to see Him happy. So the enemy approached God's children, receivers of His giving, and deceived them into thinking his way. When God's children disobeyed His laws, they set Satan's laws into motion for themselves.

No longer was God able to fellowship with them or give them His blessings. Physical deterioration set in and they began to die. Material shortage and poverty also developed. Their alienation from God was the whole cause. God's children were now prodigals—living in a hog pen.

I think if God ever cried, it had to be on this day, and then again on the day of His only begotten Son's crucifixion when He paid the price to restore what man had lost.

# God's Remedy

Through the awful death of Jesus, God was able to take away the sins His children had committed and restore fellowship with them. Jesus "...became poor, that ye through his poverty might be rich" (II Corinthians 8:9). He could not bear eternal separation from us. For this would mean that He no longer had a receiver to give to.

Satan came to steal, kill and destroy (John 10:10). But Jesus came to bind the strong man. Being stronger, Jesus took the spoil from Satan, divided it and gave it back to us (Luke 11:22). What Satan stole—fellowship with our Father, health for our bodies and prosperity in the material realm—the Lord restored to us.

Just how much does God desire to give good things to His Children? Remember, Jesus said, "Fear not, little flock; for it is your Father's good pleasure to give you the kingdom" (Luke 12:32). He desires to give good things to His children.

# Four Illustrations

Watching Jesus is the best way to observe the nature of God. Jesus declared, "...He that hath seen me hath seen the Father..." (John 14:9). Now consider with me four illustrations from the life of Jesus.

## 1. The Woman at the Well

In John 4:1-42, while the disciples were gone into Samaria to buy groceries, Jesus waited for them by Jacob's well outside of town. A woman approached the well to draw water. To get a conversation started, Jesus asked her for a drink. Surprised that Jesus would speak to her, a lowly Samaritan, she questioned why He, a Jew, would talk with her.

Notice immediately what Jesus' purpose in speaking to her was, "...If you knew...who it is that asks you for a drink—who it is that is speaking to you—you would have asked him for a drink and he would have given you living water" (John 4:10, paraphrased). He started a conversation with her so He could *give to her.*

Curious, this woman opened up her heart, and Jesus poured His words of living water into her life. She became so spiritually full that she took off running back toward the town. In her excitement, she forgot her water pots of natural water.

This woman began crying out to everyone she met, "Come, see a man who told me everything I ever did. He told me all things: (John 4:29, paraphrased). Although she had five previous husbands and was living now as a common-law wife with a sixth man, no man had ever been able to satisfy her true thirst...until she met Jesus.

Observe the conversation that followed, as Jesus and the disciples discussed what had happened. The disciples returned just in time to see the woman running away in excitement. They were shocked that Jesus had conversed with her, but hesitated to question Him about it.

However, when the disciples invited Jesus to eat He replied, **"...I have food to eat that you know nothing about"** (John 4:32, NIV). They suspicioned one another and wondered among themselves who had brought Him food. They were always competing with each other, trying to gain special favor.

Notice the revealing statement Jesus made as He explained what He meant, "...My meat—that which satisfies

My appetite—is to do the will of him that sent me, and to finish his work" (John 4:34, paraphrased). **Jesus' appetite was satisfied when He gave to that woman.** Think about the time and effort He put forth in convincing her to receive from Him.

Do you see it?

**It is not what Jesus *receives from us* that satisfies Him but what He can *convince us to receive from Him*.**

Didn't Jesus say, "...It is more blessed to *give* than to *receive*" (Acts 20:35)? Let this scripture soak in! Meditate on it! Jesus is describing the nature of God.

## 2. Mary and Martha

Luke 10:38-42 tells of a visit Jesus made to the home of Lazarus and his sisters Mary and Martha.

While Jesus and Lazarus were apparently in conversation, the women were busily preparing a meal for their special Guest. However, Mary must have been listening to their conversation from around the corner in the kitchen. Suddenly, she forgot about the meal and sat at the feet of Jesus, intently listening to His every word. "Never man spake like this man" (John 7:46).

Martha, missing her sister, realized that she was left alone to cook. Indignant, Martha approached Jesus asking Him to rebuke Mary for not helping prepare the meal. Martha naturally **assumed** that feeding Jesus was top priority.

However, she was shocked when Jesus responded: "...Martha, Martha, thou art careful and troubled about many things: But one thing is needful: and Mary hath chosen that good part, which shall not be taken away from her" (Luke 10 41-42).

Do you see it?

It was not *their* serving him that Jesus wanted. **He desired to serve *them*.**

Do you realize that it hurts the Father when He cannot freely give us all things (I Corinthians 2:12)? This certainly has top priority over His desire for us to do things for Him. You must do all you can for Him, for that is His nature working in you. However, also **let Jesus do all He wants to do for *you*,** that He may be fulfilled.

## 3. The Two Men on the Road to Emmaus

In Luke 24: 13–32 Jesus met two disciples walking from Jerusalem to Emmaus, about a six-mile walk. These men were filled with sorrow and disappointment over the crucifixion and burial of Jesus.

Not knowing that Jesus had risen, they thought His body had been stolen by the soldiers. All their hope that Jesus was the Messiah was gone. As far as they were concerned, they might as well be dead, too.

However, as they discussed these happenings, Jesus suddenly joined them but they did not recognize Him. Entering the conversation, He started quoting the Old Testament passages that predicted these events, beginning with the prophets through to that present day.

Time passed quickly. The men were enthralled by Jesus' words, but did not yet know that He was the Lord. Upon reaching their destination at Emmaus, they refused to let Him pass on. They insisted that He eat with them there. Jesus agreed.

As they sat down to their meal, Jesus lifted His hands to bless the bread. Suddenly they recognized that He was the Lord.

Now, notice what Jesus did. He disappeared! That's right. **Before He even ate,** Jesus disappeared. Why? Because

He had received His fulfillment. His satisfaction came from *giving to them*. Look at the time and effort He gave in opening them up to receive from Him. Jesus had walked and talked with them for six miles from Jerusalem to Emmaus.

**It wasn't *their* serving Him that Jesus needed. It was serving *them* that satisfied His appetite.**

Do you see it?

God gets His joy out of giving us what we need. Those men were filled with ecstacy! His joy had eliminated their sorrow. This satisfied Jesus' appetite.

## 4. The Prodigal Son

In Luke 15:11-32 Jesus told the gripping and fascinating story of a father who had two sons. The younger asked for his inheritance and left home. The elder brother stayed and continued working the fields.

Now the younger son squandered his inheritance in wanton, sinful living. Finally he ended up in a hog pen, scrapping with the pigs to get a bite to eat. As he thought back on the life he left, he realized he had made an awful mistake. However, his pride held him to the hog pen until he was languid, depleted and broken in health.

Sick, broke and destitute he finally made his decision, "I will go back to my father and ask if I can live in the servant's quarters. I will plead for mercy, and ask just to be a servant." He remembered how even the servants lived with plenty of food and surplus to spare.

The weak, young man struggled to his feet, his eyes filled with emptiness and his shoulders drooping. His clothes, reeking with stench, were now ragged and hanging in shreds. He dragged himself with worn-out shoes and bleeding feet from the hog pen. Struggling along, he finally arrived at the top of the hill overlooking his old home place.

Now his father, who had watched for him daily, saw his son's silhouette against the sky. Leaping to his feet, he ran through the yard, across the brook and up the long hill shouting, "My son, my son, you have come back!" As he ran, tears of joy blew across his cheeks.

**The Unworthy Mentality.** The boy, throwing up his hands in great embarrassment, protested, "Oh, no! I do not deserve to be a son. Please, just let me be a servant." (At times, we have all felt unworthy to be called the children of God. Perhaps you feel unworthy right now. I want you to know that God has something special just to celebrate YOUR homecoming!)

The father prevailed. Speaking over his shoulder to the servants, he shouted, "Kill the fatted calf! Bring the robe of righteousness! Get that ring of sonship! And bring shoes of service for his bleeding feet!"

As he hugged and kissed his prodigal son, the father could not contain his joy, "My son, you were dead, but now you have come back to life! My son! My son!"

**Elder Brother Mentality.** The servants killed the fatted calf and arranged the feast. The music and dancing were in full swing by the time the elder son came in from working the field. His hands were like leather from his daily chores. His skin was deeply tanned, a testimony to his faithful service in the fields day after day.

Surprised by the great rejoicing, he queried, "What is it with all this music and dancing?" A servant informed him of his brother's return and his father's killing of the fatted calf in celebration.

"He did what?" the elder brother replied in great anger. "My father killed the fatted calf for that wasteful, undeserving, unappreciative little brother of mine? I will not be a party to *that* party." Upon hearing about his eldest son's reaction, the father left the celebration and went to ask him to join the party.

The son responded furiously, "I have served you faithfully over these years, and you never gave me a goat to make merry with my friends. But as soon as this my younger brother has returned, you killed for him the fatted calf."

The father was crushed, but answered, "Son, you are always with me, and all that I have is yours" (Luke 15: 31, NKJV).

Do you know what the elder brother's problem was? *He never asked! Never asked!*

But if he *had* asked, he probably would have asked for a *goat*. Why do I say that? Because he was *goat minded!* Meanwhile, the younger brother was *unworthy minded.* Neither is the way God thinks.

Read the above paragraph again. The elder brother was **goat minded,** because he thought only in terms of *receiving the minimum.* Consequently, he **resented and persecuted** those who received his father's best—the fatted calf.

The younger brother was **unworthy minded.** He was willing to settle for *even less than the minimum!* He felt unworthy to receive. Scraps were good enough for him.

**Fat-Calf Mentality.** Now consider the father's mentality. The father was *fat-calf minded.* He was disappointed in the elder son when he refused to come in and partake of what the father had provided. The father thought in terms of *only* the best for his heirs.

We must accept our position as *sons* and *heirs* of God. Then will we serve Him well. Only then can we have the proper attitude to receive what he desperately desires to give us.

Someone said it this way: **"God always gives His best to those who leave the choice with Him."**

> **Fear not, little flock; for it is your Father's good pleasure to give you the kingdom.**
>
> **Luke 12:32**

We need to change our traditional thinking if we are ever going to live according to God's will. "For as a man thinketh in his heart, so is he" (Proverbs 23:7, paraphrased).

Does the Father have a need? Oh, yes! And His need will not be satisfied until you open up and let Him give to you His best.

Are you **unworthy minded** thinking you are undeserving? Or **goat minded** thinking in terms of minimums? Or are you **fat-calf minded** thinking like God thinks?

*Do you think like the Father?* The Bible says to "Let this mind be in you, which was also in Christ Jesus" (Philippians 2:5). **Learn to think like God.**

He desperately desires to give His best to you. Jesus said, "Herein is my father glorified, that ye bear much fruit; so shall ye be my disciples" (John 15:8).

## Summary

*It is not what He receives from us that satisfies God, but what He can convince us to receive from Him.*

The **carnal nature** loves to receive, but the **spiritual nature** loves to give. Choose to walk according to the spiritual nature God has given you. Receive His best. Then look for ways to give Him to others.

"If we live in the Spirit, let us also walk in the Spirit" (Galatians 5:25).

# 2

# Prosperity by Default

What is "prosperity by default"? Maybe you have never heard this phrase. At first it may sound strange, but this is how you and I receive the promises of God. To help you understand the concept of prosperity by default, let me first explain "salvation by grace" and "God's mercy."

## What Is the Difference between God's Grace and His Mercy?

Salvation of your soul is a gift from God. You do not *deserve* it. You cannot receive it by your deeds or goodness. What, then, causes God to give such a gift? It is *by His grace through your faith* that you are saved.

> ...**By grace are ye saved** *through faith*....
>
> **Ephesians 2:8**

> **Therefore it is** *of faith,* **that it might be** *by* **grace....**
>
> **Romans 4:16**

**By whom also we have *access by faith* into this grace.**
**Romans 5:2**

From these Scriptures, you can see that it is your faith that releases God's grace. Through your faith, you obtain His grace to receive salvation. God counts your faith **as righteousness.** Therefore He views you as **worthy** (through your faith in the blood of Jesus). He **"counts you worthy"** and looks at you as though you *deserved* salvation.

> ...Abraham believed God, and it was counted unto him for righteousness.
> ...To him that...believeth on him that justifieth the ungodly, *his faith is counted for righteousness.*
> **Romans 4:3, 5**

In other words, *because* of your faith, God bestows His grace upon you, which means that you find favor with Him. This grace is not unmerited in His eyes; it is because of your faith. He responds to your faith by granting you the gift of righteousness—not because of your goodness, but because Jesus purchased it for you at Calvary. You appropriate this gift of righteousness through your faith. So now when God looks at you, He sees only the righteousness of Jesus. Because of the blood of Jesus, you are counted as worthy and deserving of salvation.

**Mercy,** on the other hand, is God's *unmerited* favor. Romans 9:15 tells us that God will have mercy on whom He will have mercy. In other words, in His sovereign will, God decides where and when He will pour out His mercy upon people.

While mercy is unpredictable, grace is absolutely predictable. Grace comes only to those whom God counts worthy because of their faith: "...According to your faith be it [grace] unto you" (Matthew 9:29).

# We Receive All God's Promises by Grace through Faith

Since you receive the gift of salvation by grace through faith, let's consider God's other gifts in the same light.

**Beloved, I wish above all things that thou mayest prosper and be in health,** *even as thy soul prospereth.*
**III John 2**

Unless God heals you as an act of mercy, healing for your physical body comes by grace through faith. But this does not stop with the physical. It also applies to your material supply. Think with me as we consider it graphically.

## How to Possess the Wealth of the Sinner

God has made some very vivid statements illustrating His desires for your material supply. In various ways throughout His Word, God tells you that "the wealth of the sinner is laid up for the just" (Proverbs 13:22). Obviously He would not have made this statement unless He meant for you to possess the sinner's wealth. But how do you obtain it? Let's see.

Notice in Deuteronomy 9:1-6, that God encouraged the Children of Israel to aggressively move into the land He had promised them—a land filled with milk and honey, and grapes the size of grapefruit. However, concerning the giants and enemies in that Promised Land, God instructed:

> ...The Lord thy God is he which goeth over before thee; as a consuming fire he shall destroy them, and he shall bring them down before thy face: so shalt thou drive them out, and destroy them quickly, as the Lord hath said unto thee.
>
> Speak not thou in thine heart...saying, For my righteousness the Lord hath brought me in to possess this land: *but for the wickedness of these nations the Lord doth drive them out....*
>
> Deuteronomy 9:3-4

Here, it is clear that the Children of Israel would possess the wealth of the wicked in their Promised Land. However, God would give this prosperity to His children not because of their own righteousness, but **because of the wickedness of the other nations.**

> Not for thy righteousness, or for the uprightness of thine heart, dost thou go to possess *their land:* but for the wickedness of these nations the Lord thy God doth drive them out from before thee....
>
> Understand therefore, that the Lord thy God giveth thee not this good land to possess it for thy righteousness; for thou art a stiffnecked people.
>
> Deuteronomy 9:5-6

The other nations *did not* use their wealth to please God, so He wanted to give it to His covenant people, whom He called "stiffnecked." **Did His people deserve this prosperity because of their goodness or deeds?** Obviously not. **They received it because others had not used it properly.**
*This is prosperity by default.*
Although they did not deserve it, the Jews received

other people's prosperity by God's grace because these other nations had defaulted and failed God. However, God promised to give this wealth to the Children of Israel *only if they exercised their faith and moved toward it.* They could receive it by grace but **only through their faith.**

This is also true of possessing *your* Promised Land—the wealth of the wicked.

- If you don't believe *in* it, you won't believe *for* it.
- If you don't believe for it, you won't move toward it.
- And if you don't move toward it, you won't have it.

## You, Too, Can Lose Your Prosperity by Default

The Jews received the prosperity of the sinner by default. But what did they do with it? God warned His people that they, too, could lose their prosperity by default.

> **And it shall be, if thou do at all forget the Lord thy God, and walk after other gods [in this case, the love of money and the lust of the flesh instead of His purpose and pursuits], and serve them, and worship them, I testify against you this day that ye shall surely perish.**
>
> **As the nations which the Lord destroyeth before your face, so shall ye perish; because ye would not be obedient unto the voice of the Lord your God.**
>
> **Deuteronomy 8:19-20**

Now let me ask you this: Did the Jews, God's covenant people, default? Did they turn aside from the Word of God and deserve to perish, according to this Scripture? **They did!** Not only were they stiffnecked and rebellious in the wilderness, but they rejected God's voice sent to this earth in the person of Jesus Christ, His Son.

They definitely defaulted.

In Matthew 21:42-43, we have Jesus' own words in reference to this default.

> Jesus saith unto them, Did ye never read in the scriptures, The stone which the builders rejected, the same is become the head of the corner: this is the Lord's doing, and it is marvellous in our eyes?
>
> Therefore say I unto you, The kingdom of God shall be taken from you, and given to a nation bringing forth the fruits thereof.
>
> Matthew 21:42-43

Their default opened the door for others to receive *their* prosperity. Look at what the Apostle Paul declared about this default of the Jews:

> I say then, Have they stumbled that they should fall? God forbid: but rather through their fall salvation is come unto the Gentiles, for to provoke them to jealousy.
>
> Now if the fall of them be the riches of the world, and the diminishing of them the riches of the Gentiles; how much more their fulness?
>
> For I speak to you Gentiles, inasmuch as I am the apostle of the Gentiles, I magnify mine office:
>
> If by any means I may provoke to emulation them which are my flesh, and might save some of them.
>
> For if the casting away of them be the reconciling of the world, what shall the receiving of them be, but life from the dead?
>
> For if the firstfruit be holy, the lump is also holy: and if the root be holy, so are the branches.
>
> And if some of the branches be broken off, and thou, being a wild olive tree, wert graffed in among them, and with them partakest of the root and fatness of the olive tree;

> Boast not against the branches. But if thou boast, thou barest not the root, but the root thee.
>
> Thou wilt say then, The branches were broken off, that I might be graffed in.
>
> Well; because of unbelief they were broken off, and thou standest by faith. Be not highminded, but fear:
>
> For if God spared not the natural branches, take heed lest he also spare not thee.
>
> Behold therefore the goodness and severity of God: on them which fell, severity; but toward thee, goodness, if thou continue in his goodness: otherwise thou also shalt be cut off.
>
> Romans 11:11-22

Now, assuming that everyone in Paul's day was aware of the Jews' default, he asked: "...Have they stumbled that they should fall? God forbid: but...*through their fall salvation is come unto the Gentiles...*" (Romans 11:11).

God didn't annihilate His covenant people, the Jews. However, their default opened a cleavage in the trunk of the olive tree (symbolic of the Hebrew nation), so we Gentiles could be grafted in and become **partakers of the root and fatness of that tree.**

Paul states their fall became "the riches of the Gentiles," and their casting away became "the reconciling of the world" (Romans 11:12, 15).

Are we Gentiles to boast then, that because of our own goodness God brought us into the blessings of the Jews? No! We didn't get in on their covenant riches because we deserved it, but only because the Jews defaulted. We obtain it by God's grace through our faith.

The Jews' unbelief caused them to be broken off. This opened the door to us to be grafted in **by faith.** But just like He warned *them* in Deuteronomy 8, God warns *us* that we, too, can lose our prosperity by default:

> **For if God spared not the natural branches, take heed lest he also spare not thee.**
> **Romans 11:21**

God will pass by a million unbelievers in search of one person who believes. This is the one to whom He will give His promises.

> **Behold therefore the goodness and severity of God: on them which fell [doubted], severity; but toward thee [those who stand in faith for it], goodness, IF thou CONTINUE in his goodness: otherwise thou also shalt be cut off.**
> **Romans 11:22**

So then, by God's grace through our faith, we are now heirs of a new Promised Land (new covenant blessings). But not because of our righteousness. *It is because of the righteousness of Jesus Christ, which is passed on to us through faith and by grace.* Paul summarized it this way:

> **...Abraham believed God, and it was counted unto him for righteousness.**
> **But to him [you, the believer] that... believeth on him [Jesus Christ] that justifieth the ungodly, his faith is counted for righteousness.**
> **For the promise, that he should be the heir of the world, was...to Abraham...[and] to his seed [that's you!]...through the righteousness of faith.**
> **Therefore it is of faith, that it might be by grace; to the end the promise might be sure to all the seed...of Abraham; who is the father of us all,**
> **He staggered not at the promise of God through unbelief; but was strong in faith, giving glory to God;**

And being fully persuaded that, what he had promised, he was able also to perform.

And therefore it was imputed to him for righteousness.

Now it was not written for his sake alone...

But for us also, to whom it shall be imputed, if we
believe on him that raised up Jesus our Lord from the dead;

Who was delivered for our offences, and was raised
again for our justification.

Romans 4:3, 5, 13, 16, 20-25

Through our belief in Jesus Christ, by God's grace, we
are heirs of the new Promised Land.

## Observe the Abundance

Now let's look at the prosperity of the Children of Israel
into which we as believing Gentiles have been grafted. This
is what our new Promised Land is like.

In Deuteronomy 8:7-13, God called the Promised Land,
Canaan, a good land filled with plenty of brooks and foun-
tains—a land of wheat and barley, fig trees, vines, pome-
granates, olive oil, and honey. God called it a land where
they could "eat bread without scarceness." They could eat
until they were filled. It was a land where they would **not
lack anything.**

In this land, He said they could build "good houses"
and dwell in them. I view that to mean mortgage-free. He
also told them that their herds and flocks would multiply, as
well as their **silver** and **gold**—money.

Then God summarized all their blessings by saying,
"...all that thou hast is multiplied..." (Deuteronomy 8:13).

Notice God's nature here. He wants to multiply good

gifts to His children. This Scripture reminds me of Proverbs 10:22, which says something very powerful of God.

**The blessing of the Lord, it maketh rich, and he addeth** *no sorrow with it.*

**Proverbs 10:22**

When you let God do your arithmetic, He uses addition and multiplication. But when you let Satan do your arithmetic, he uses subtraction and division.

**The thief cometh not, but for to steal, and to kill, and to destroy.**

**John 10:10**

Deuteronomy 8:18 says, "But thou shalt remember the Lord thy God: for it is he that giveth thee *power to get wealth,* that he may *establish his covenant....*" **God's obvious purpose in giving His children power to get wealth is so that we, who are seeking first the kingdom of God, will have ample funds to carry out the redeeming of all humanity.** God knows we will need plenty of money to do that. Remember, He also gets pleasure out of giving good things to His children. (See Psalm 37.)

**Fear not, little flock; for it is your Father's good pleasure to give you the kingdom.**

**Luke 12:32**

**Who satisfieth thy mouth with good things; so that thy youth is renewed like the eagle's.**

**Psalm 103:5**

At this point, I hope that you are beginning to feel your faith rising to start moving aggressively toward your Promised Land. I want to encourage you to let your faith soar. If God sees FAITH in your heart, He has ways of getting riches into your hands. He is the One Who does it. Listen for good ideas from God.

- **Seek** God first.
- **Obey** God's instructions.
- **Believe** aggressively for your Promised Land.
- **Talk** like you believe.
- **Look** for it.
- **Do** things that you think might generate it.
- **Be generous** and liberal, above all, in your giving because "the liberal soul shall be made fat" (Proverbs 11:25).

## Five Witnesses

Now I want to show you five Scriptures that will boost your faith. These will help you to start aggressively believing God to take His wealth from the ungodly and give it to you, a believer.

"In the mouth of two or three witnesses shall every word [doctrine] be established" (II Corinthians 13:1). Below are five witnesses:

> ...Now thus saith the Lord that created thee...he that formed thee...Fear not: for I have redeemed thee, I have called thee by thy name; thou art mine.
>
> When thou passest through the waters, I will be with thee; and through the rivers, they shall not overflow thee: when thou walkest through the fire, thou shalt not be burned; neither shall the flame kindle upon thee.

> ...*I gave* Egypt for *thy ransom,* Ethiopia and Sheba for thee.
>
> ...I have loved thee: therefore will *I give men for thee, and people for thy life.*
>
> **Isaiah 43:1-4**

> The wicked shall be a RANSOM for the righteous, and the transgressor for the upright.
>
> **Proverbs 21:18**

> For God giveth to a man that is good in his sight wisdom, knowledge, and joy: but to the sinner he giveth travail, *to gather and to heap up,* that he may *give to him* that is good before God.
>
> **Ecclesiastes 2:26**

Travail is all God gives the sinner, but to His children God gives an "easy yoke and light burden" (Matthew 11:30). You don't have "to rise up early, to sit up late, to eat the bread of sorrows" to make it in this world (Psalm 127:2). God has a better plan for His people. Can you believe for it? Here are two more Scriptures that bear witness to this truth:

> This is the portion of a wicked man with God, and the heritage of oppressors, which they shall receive of the Almighty.
>
> Though he heap up silver as the dust [abundant money], and prepare raiment as the clay;
>
> He may prepare it, *but the just shall put it on,* and the innocent shall divide the silver.
>
> **Job 27:13, 16, 17**

> Rest in the Lord and wait patiently for him....
>
> For evildoers shall be cut off: but those that wait upon

**the Lord, they** *shall inherit the earth.*

**Psalms 37:7, 9**

## The Wealth of the Sinner Is Laid up for YOU!

God illustrated this principle or truth to me one Monday morning when I drove to a convenience store to buy gasoline. Earlier, I had paid all my bills and tithes, and had shared an offering at church. But now I only had two dollars in my pocket and a full week ahead of me before I was scheduled to preach again or receive any money. At that time, I had no partners sending in support, and I had no money in reserve. Neither did I have any credit cards.

As I drove up to the pump, I prayed a short prayer, "Father, I need some gas and running money for this week. You are the only Source I can turn to. I look to You for my supply. Thanks for doing something."

I pumped two dollars worth of gasoline and went inside to empty my pockets to pay the bill. There was a line of about four or five people ahead of me. When it was my turn, I paid the cashier and turned to walk out the door. Looking down, I noticed a roll of $20 bills laying at my feet. I reached down and picked it up, and looked around to see if anyone was looking for them. However, nearly everyone had left the premises, and there was no wallet, purse, or checkbook attached to them.

I stood there wondering how to find the owner, when suddenly I heard a still, small voice inside me, "You asked Me for money to run the rest of the week. **A wicked person dropped this on the way out, and I kept it there for you.**" I suddenly remembered the previous verses. (God knows that if there would have been a way to find the owner, I would have. But there was not.)

I went out to the car and unfolded the money, and counted seven $20 bills—$140 was a lot of money back then! I thanked the Lord and went on my way with enough spending money to last the entire week.

I wonder if Peter struggled to find the owner of the money he found in the fish's mouth. Some wealthy person lost it, and Jesus told Peter where it was. It was a lot of money. It paid the annual taxes for Jesus and Peter's household. (See Matthew 17:24-27.)

Did you ever wonder where the bread came from that the ravens brought Elijah twice a day for nearly two years while he sat in the desert by the brook? It probably came from wicked King Ahab's bakery. He is the most likely one to have any food during the famine. (See I Kings 17.)

Since my experience of finding the money, the Lord has blessed us so we don't run that close. But you and I have the reassurance that when the Lord is looking out for us, He is our security. Do we deserve it? Not in our eyes, but by His grace God sees us worthy when we walk in faith.

You must trust Him to make provision for your every need. However, it is extremely important that you **do not pursue the provisions.** Do not pursue the wealth of others. You must not pursue fame and prosperity in the natural realm. Instead, pursue God. Focus upon Him. Listen to His voice. Obey Him.

As you do what God instructs you to do, He will do what He promised you. He will bring money from unexpected sources when you need it. He will give you favor wherever you go. God will direct your steps to find all that He has for you...**but** you must keep your eyes on Him, not His gifts. His gifts are byproducts of your obedience; they are not to be your goals.

In other words, you are not to pursue God's provisions from the sources He uses. God Himself is to do this. You see, there are certain things that are legal for God but illegal for us to do. For example, we are not to take vengeance for ourselves. God said, "...'Vengeance is Mine; I will repay....The Lord will judge His people'" (Hebrews 10:30, NKJV). Likewise, we are not to go looking for things to take from others to bless ourselves.

God is the Judge. It is up to His discretion as to how and when He will bless us. We are not to take matters into our own hands by seeking it ourselves. Instead, the Bible instructs us to prefer one another before self—not rendering evil for evil, but good for evil (Romans 12:10; I Peter 3:9).

# Summary

In short, it is not wrong to obtain things from others, but it *is* wrong for us to take them ourselves. If someone is not using something for God's glory, He will take it from that person and give it to those who *will* use it for His glory.

A clear example of this is found in II Kings 7, the story of the four lepers. Because a famine had struck Israel, four lepers were discussing how they could survive. Despite the great odds against them, these four men rose up in faith to go forward into the enemy's camp.

What they didn't know was that God had made the Syrian enemy hear the sounds of a great army rushing toward them. The Syrians immediately fled in fear of their very lives, leaving all their tents filled with silver, gold, clothes, food and other valuables. When the four lepers arrived at the camp, they discovered God's miracle. The vast abundance was totally left for them. Not only were their personal needs met, but because they shared the abundance with others, their obedience instantly ended the famine for the entire city.

As a child of God, you, too, are entitled to the abundance of the sinner. To possess *your* Promised Land, I repeat:

- **Seek** God first.
- **Obey** God's instructions.
- **Believe** aggressively for your Promised Land.
- **Talk** like you believe.
- **Look** for it.
- **Do** things that you think might generate it.
- **Be generous** and liberal, above all, in your giving because "the liberal soul shall be made fat" (Proverbs 11:25).

Call yourself as God calls you: worthy, not unworthy... rich not poor. Walk in His grace by faith. You are His child and, therefore, an heir of **His abundant grace.**

# 3

# The Prosperity of Fools

Many warnings about money can be found throughout Scripture. In Proverbs 1:32, for example, Solomon notes that "...the prosperity of fools shall destroy them."

In this chapter, you will learn how to avoid the destruction that prosperity brings to fools. This is of utmost importance. It is the hinge from which all other chapters in this book swing. Study it thoroughly.

I was born in a Christian home in which spiritual values were emphasized at each turn. From this admirable position, a withdrawal from any material interest evolved. My family always pointed out the dangers of "possessing things lest they possess you." This valuable truth came from the important warnings about riches in Scripture.

Let's take a look at some of these. One of the strongest warnings concerning the negative influence of riches is found in Deuteronomy 32.

> For the Lord's portion is his people; Jacob is the lot of his inheritance.
>
> He found him in a desert land, and in the waste howling wilderness; he led him about, he instructed him, he kept him as the apple of his eye.

As an eagle stirreth up her nest, fluttereth over her young, spreadeth abroad her wings, taketh them, beareth them on her wings:

So the Lord alone did lead him, and there was no strange god with him.

He made him ride on the high places of the earth, that he might eat the increase of the fields; and he made him to suck honey out of the rock, and oil out of the flinty rock;

Butter of kine, and milk of sheep, with fat of lambs, and rams of the breed of Bashan, and goats, with the fat of kidneys of wheat; and thou didst drink the pure blood of the grape.

But Jeshurun waxed fat, and kicked: thou art waxen fat, thou art grown thick, thou art covered with fatness; then he forsook God which made him, and lightly esteemed the Rock of his salvation.

Deuteronomy 32:9-15

God begins this passage by telling us that "the Lord's portion is his people." God loves His children and delights in blessing them. Verses 13 and 14, describe how He blessed Jeshurun (a poetic term for Israel) with an abundance of material supply to "ride on the high places of the earth, that he might eat the increase of the fields; and...to suck honey out of the rock...Butter of kine [cows]...with fat of lambs, and ...with the fat of kidneys of wheat; and...drink the pure blood of the grape [undiluted]." Then, however, verse 15 reveals how Jeshurun forsook God.

This is a classic example of how material abundance can ruin your relationship with God. The sinister temptation in the abundance of material provision is **self-sufficiency.** This sin leads a person or nation away from dependency on God. A false sense of security lurks beneath the surface of material abundance. Hence, the many warnings in Scripture.

> ...If riches increase, set not your heart upon them.
> **Psalm 62:10**

> He that trusteth in his riches shall fall....
> **Proverbs 11:28**

> He that loveth silver shall not be satisfied with silver; nor he that loveth abundance with increase: this is also vanity.
> **Ecclesiastes 5:10**

> ...Yet is there no end of all his labour; neither is his eye satisfied with riches....This is also vanity, yea, it is a sore travail.
> **Ecclesiastes 4:8**

Riches and abundance of things do not make a person happy. They promise it, but they don't fulfill the promise. Consider Jeremiah 9:23, "...Let not the rich man glory in his...riches."

Jesus taught us in Matthew 13:22 that the deceitfulness of riches chokes the Word and becomes unfruitful. Notice: The problem wasn't riches, but the **deceitfulness** of riches.

## The Disciples' Shock

Consider Jesus' message in the book of Mark concerning the deceitfulness of riches:

> And Jesus looked round about, and saith unto his disciples, How hardly shall they that have riches enter into the kingdom of God!
> And the disciples were astonished at his words. But

> **Jesus answereth again, and saith unto them, Children, how hard is it for them that trust in riches to enter into the kingdom of God!**
>
> **It is easier for a camel to go through the eye of a needle, than for a rich man to enter into the kingdom of God.**
> **Mark 10:23-25**

Continuing on to verse 26, this passage shows how shocked the disciples were at Jesus' statement, "...They were astonished *out of measure*...." The disciples were surprised because they had observed how rich people gravitated to Jesus and supported His ministry. How could it be difficult for them to enter into the kingdom of God? These rich people were such close followers of Jesus. Before I answer this question, let me explain something critical about riches.

## Jesus Had Plenty of Money

It is important for you to understand that Jesus did not become poor according to the world's level of poverty. He became poor relative to His riches in glory. This He did that God might "...supply all your need **according to his riches in glory**..." (Philippians 4:19). Owning enough riches to have all your needs met is not a sin. In fact, Jesus had earthly riches.

There is no record where Jesus ever passed an offering plate, though it is certainly scriptural to do so (I Corinthians 9:9-14). Yet, Jesus had plenty of money to do His work. You see, those whom Jesus helped, blessed and healed began supporting His ministry. So much support was coming in that Jesus appointed Judas as His full-time treasurer. Judas even stole from the ministry's treasury bag, and nobody seemed to know—except Jesus.

We know, of course, that Jesus and the disciples did not *steal* anything to add to the ministry's treasury. There are only two records of Jesus *multiplying food* (Matthew 14:14-21 and 15:32-38), and one record of their *buying victuals (groceries)* in Sychar (John 4:5, 8). Obviously, there was more than enough money in the bag to support the work of the ministry.

Additionally, with no other sources of income, there was enough money in Judas's bag to feed and clothe Jesus' staff of twelve disciples and their families for three years. Could you do that if you weren't sufficiently supplied with money? Remember, Matthew had left his tax collecting job; Peter, James and John had left their nets; and others had done the same. All twelve disciples ministered full-time, and the ministry supported them as they constantly followed Jesus (except for brief visits at home with relatives). Jesus had money.

Now this isn't hard for me to understand, because Jesus taught that when you give, it comes back to you according to the measure with which you gave—"good measure, pressed down, and shaken together, and running over..." (Luke 6:38). Based on His own teaching, Jesus had more than enough for His ministry because He gave regularly to the poor. This is why Mark 12:37 states that the common people "heard him gladly." Jesus ministered both physically, spiritually and materially to the poor.

Solomon said in Proverbs 28:27, "He that giveth unto the poor **shall not lack...**" and Jesus was the greatest giver to ever come along. His ministry's finances did not lack.

If Jesus' teachings didn't work for Him, how can you expect them to work for you?

# Jesus Was Supported from Herod's Treasure

Luke 8:1-3 gives us the record of how certain women followed Jesus daily, ministering to Him of their substance. One of these women was Joanna, wife of Chuza, who was the steward of King Herod. Even King Herod was unknowingly supporting Jesus' ministry out of his abundant treasury!

The disciples knew all of this and were confused at Jesus' statement about it being difficult for rich people to enter into the kingdom of God. That is why Jesus explained to them, "...With men it is impossible, but not with God: for with God all things are possible" (Mark 10:27).

In other words, it would take a miracle for a rich person to get saved, but God can do it. However, we know that it takes a miracle to save any of us. So why did Jesus make a distinction about the salvation of the rich? Obviously, it was because first they must do something very difficult: abandon their "trust in riches."

The poor man does not struggle with this problem. However, of course, the poor man also does not have the ability to sponsor the ministry of Jesus. He is only a receiver. Because of this, the poor man misses out on the great blessing of giving. (Remember, in Acts 20:35, Jesus said it is "more blessed to give.")

So how do we resolve this? Should we desire to be rich or poor, or simply somewhere in between?

- To be rich is to suffer the temptations that go with riches, yet experience the blessing of giving.
- To be poor is to miss the joy of giving, but not face the temptations of having riches. However, to be poor also means to be subservient to the rich and to be under their control. (Proverbs 22:7 says, "The rich

ruleth over the poor, and the borrower is servant to the lender.")

## Sponsors of the Gospel

The Word clearly answers this dilemma. It instructs us, "We then that are strong ought to bear the infirmities of the weak..." (Romans 15:1). We cannot do this if we are also weak and without money.

Of course, the *ungodly* are not likely to voluntarily sponsor the Gospel. So, there is only one category of people interested in doing this—the *godly*. However, if we, God's children, are supposed to avoid abundance, how can we help the weak and thereby fulfill the Great Commission?

## God Needs Money

Personally, I have made 23 missionary journeys out of this country, and I know firsthand that it requires a great deal of money. God tells us in Deuteronomy 8:18 that He gave us, His heritage, the "power to get wealth" so He can establish His covenant.

God needs money to support His work in the earth. In fact, He requests it and commands it.

> Bring ye all the tithes into the storehouse, *that there may be meat in mine house,* and prove me now herewith, saith the Lord of hosts, if I will not open you the windows of heaven, and pour you out a blessing, that there shall not be room enough to receive it.
>
> **Malachi 3:10**

It requires **money** to get God's work done.

- The **more** money you have, the **more** of God's work you can do.
- The **less** you have, the **less** you can do.

What, then, are you to do with this prosperity issue? Is it God's will, or is it not?

## Don't Be a Fool

In my 39 years of ministry, several times I have heard people say, "God knows He can't give me much money. He knows I couldn't handle it." They probably are not far from the truth of the matter. God knows all things. I believe that God will not sacrifice the salvation of a soul by giving him money that would destroy him—even if it takes money to reach other unsaved souls. God finds others who *will* support His work.

Remember, "the prosperity of fools shall destroy them" (Proverbs 1:32). A fool is any person who is deceived by riches. He trusts in riches more than he desires to please God. Because a fool is obsessed with money, he will go to great lengths to obtain more riches. He will even violate a good conscience and the Word of God, for example, by not tithing. Don't be a fool.

God desires to "freely give us [His children] all things" (Romans 8:32). You and I are God's heritage or His inheritors. If He observes that He is the first priority in our present desires and interests, then He promises, "all these things shall be added unto you" (Matthew 6:33). However, you must remember that God loves you too much to give you something that will hurt you. Don't be a fool.

# Fleshly Desires over Spiritual

Many people have heard this positive message of prosperity, and have seized it with their own interests in the forefront. It *is* possible to obtain things from God—if you are extremely persistent—only to have it be to your own hurt.

For example, when the Hebrew children, in the wilderness, cried for flesh to eat instead of their daily supply of manna (symbolic of fleshly desires over spiritual interests), Scripture records, "...He gave them their request; but sent *leanness into their soul*" (Psalm 106:15). The prosperity of these fools destroyed them.

# Top Priority

You and I must get our priorities straight. Do you think more about the things you want (material possessions), or do you sincerely desire to promote, more than any other interest, the cause of Jesus? Be honest in answering this important question.

Proverbs 1:32 says that you cannot be a fool *and* keep your prosperity. You can only have one or the other. Will you abandon prosperity in order to maintain the fool status, or will you choose to abandon the fool status to obtain prosperity?

Your answer to this question will determine whether you should continue to read the balance of this book. If you choose to abandon being a fool, then you will be especially interested in the remaining chapters of this book concerning the Christian and finances.

# The Teachings of Agur

Before I bring this very important chapter to a close, I want you to ponder Proverbs 30:7-9 with me. These particular verses of Scripture are a pattern from which many people pray. However, such people overlook a major truth in the previous verses, which has misled the neo-Christian mind. First, let's look at verses 7-9:

> Two things have I required of thee; deny me them not before I die:
> Remove far from me vanity and lies [a scriptural prayer so far]: give me neither poverty nor riches; feed me with food convenient for me:
> Lest I be full, and deny thee, and say, Who is the Lord? or lest I be poor, and steal, and take the name of my God in vain.
>
> Proverbs 30:7-9

The man speaking in these verses is King Agur, according to Proverbs 30:1. Pay close attention to the king's own description of his mental capacity in the earlier verses:

> Surely I am more stupid than any man, and do not have the understanding of a man.
> I neither learned wisdom nor have knowledge of the Holy One.
>
> Proverbs 30:2-3 (NKJV)

# Take Caution

Now, if an instructor told me, before he began his instructions, that he classified himself as stupid and that he knew that he didn't think like God, what would I do? Proceed with great caution! I would not be impressed by his advice or example. I certainly would weigh his instructions *very* carefully.

# Satan Instructs Jesus with Scripture

You are not to blindly follow every verse in the Bible. Taking Scriptures out of context can be dangerous. This is a common way the devil tries to deceive Christians.

There are several places in Scripture that teach things you should *not* follow. The prime example is in Matthew 4:5-6 where Satan instructed Jesus to cast Himself from the pinnacle of the temple and quoted Psalm 91:11 to support his suggestion.

Sometimes Satan attacks openly, but he will usually come to a Bible believer camouflaged as "an angel of light" according to II Corinthians 11:14. Discern who is speaking to you before you act upon the word spoken—even if it is Scripture.

It is important to remember that if Satan tried to confuse Jesus by quoting Scripture in an effort to move Him out of God's will, he will try to do the same to you.

In light of this, let's return to the verses regarding King Agur, who was "more stupid than any man"! He had an obvious fear of riches. He did not feel that he could handle the temptations that would come with wealth.

> ...Give me neither poverty nor riches...
>
> Lest I...deny thee, and say, Who is the Lord?...[The temptation of riches, *self-sufficiency*.]
>
> **Proverbs 30:8-9**

Neither did he want poverty. The king knew that the temptation here would be bitterness and anger, eventually leading to stealing and cursing God. King Agur knew this was a ruinous and sinful attitude, so he made His choice in verse 8: "...Give me...food convenient for me." The king settled for a position where neither the temptations of poverty or riches would exist. He asked for only enough for himself.

King Agur did not have an interest in the needs of others. He had no interest in reaching out to the poor or to the depressed. He certainly did not have a missionary vision.

In short, he chose to live in selfishness. He was not willing to face and overcome the temptations of riches in order to help someone else. He had no vision. "Where there is no vision, the people perish..." (Proverbs 29:18). Does this sound like someone whose advice you want to follow?

I admit, there are temptations in having riches, but the Word teaches us to be overcomers. **You will never overcome the temptations of riches by simply avoiding them.**

## Dangers in Sex

Let me switch to another subject for a moment to clarify my point here. Wanting a minimum of money—only enough to meet YOUR daily needs—is like a couple engaging in sex only when they want to produce a child. There are many dangers, temptations, and perversions in the area of sex. However, to say that the best posture is to avoid sex except when necessary for reproductive purposes would be ridiculous.

# Guidelines for Sex

Yes, there are many dangerous temptations in sex, but God gave this precious gift to bring great joy to mankind. However, we must practice it **only** according to His plan. That's why God gave us severe warnings and specific guidelines on the subject of sex.

# Learn the Pitfalls

The same principles apply to money. There is a ditch on both sides of these roads. Sex and money. However, God does not instruct us as Christians to avoid them, but to follow the guidelines and to stay in the middle of the road. Learn the pitfalls and traps. Be an overcomer of the temptations, so you can enjoy the full benefits of both.

# Summary

Jesus said about money, "...It is more blessed to give than to receive" (Acts 20:35). The more money we have, the more good we can do. The less money we have, the less we can accomplish. God wants us to be rich so we can help the poor. God wants us to be above so we can lift up others.

- The **more** you give, the **greater** the blessing and satisfaction.

You are to be strong and bear the infirmities of the weak, but **you cannot give in abundance if you do not have it to give.**

Abandon the fool status and believe God for an abundance, so you can be an abundant blessing. Do not let the devil give you a guilt complex. He condemns you and tries to steal from you. However, God justifies you and gives blessings to you if you expect and believe for them.

# 4

# What It Means to Be a Liberal Soul

What kind of man or woman is God looking for? Are you the type of person He is trying to find? If you are, He is about to pour out so many blessings upon you that you will not be able to contain them all!

> For the eyes of the Lord search back and forth across the whole earth, looking for people whose hearts are perfect toward him, so that he can show his great power in helping them....
>
> II Chronicles 16:9 (TLB)

## People Whom God Made Rich

Throughout Scripture, we see a pattern of God looking for, finding and then blessing faithful servants with wealth, honor and long life. Let's take a look at how God describes several of these men in His Word.

God called Abraham His "friend" (James 2:23). He blessed Abraham to become the richest man in all the land.

God described David as "a man after mine own heart" (Acts 13:22). Look how God blessed him. David was able to give over $576 million of his own money to build the temple. Still he "died in a good old age, full of days, riches, and honour" (I Chronicles 29:28).

God called Moses "very meek, above all the men which were upon the face of the earth" (Numbers 12:3). Look how God blessed him. Moses governed over 3 million people, yet he functioned in constant supernatural power.

God considered Joseph "a fruitful bough...whose branches run over the wall" (Genesis 49:22). Look how God blessed him. He placed Joseph in charge of all the money in Egypt.

God described Caleb as a man who "wholly followed the Lord" (Deuteronomy 1:36). Look how God blessed him. At age 80, Caleb first defeated and then governed the giants in the mountain zone.

God promised Joshua, "...As I was with Moses, so I will be with you..." (Joshua 1:5). Look how God blessed him. God even made the "sun stand still" for him (Joshua 10:12).

Obed-Edom, a Gentile and "an alien from the commonwealth" (Ephesians 2:12), found favor with God when he embraced God's ark of the covenant and laws (II Samuel 6:12). Look how God blessed him. In less than three months, Obed-Edom was made a rich man and the envy of all Jerusalem.

What kind of a man or woman is God looking for in order to show forth His goodness? Are you the type He is looking for? Do you desire His blessings? You must first have a heart that is "perfect toward Him."

## God Is Searching

Psalm 15 provides specific insight about what God is looking for.

Lord, who shall abide in thy tabernacle? who shall dwell in thy holy hill?

He that walketh uprightly, and worketh righteousness, and speaketh the truth in his heart.

He that backbiteth not with his tongue, nor doeth evil to his neighbour, nor taketh up a reproach against his neighbour.

In whose eyes a vile person is contemned; but he honoureth them that fear the Lord. He that sweareth to his own hurt, and changeth not.

He that putteth not out his money to usury, nor taketh reward against the innocent. He that doeth these things shall never be moved.

**Psalm 15:1-5**

The first Psalm also describes how you can have a heart that is perfect toward God. This is a good passage to memorize.

Blessed is the man that walketh not in the counsel of the ungodly, nor standeth in the way of sinners, nor sitteth in the seat of the scornful.

But his delight is in the law of the Lord; and in his law doth he meditate day and night.

And he shall be like a tree planted by the rivers of water, that bringeth forth his fruit in his season; his leaf also shall not wither; and whatsoever he doeth shall prosper.

The ungodly are not so: but are like the chaff which the wind driveth away.

Therefore the ungodly shall not stand in the judgment, nor sinners in the congregation of the righteous.

For the Lord knoweth the way of the righteous: but the way of the ungodly shall perish.

**Psalm 1:1-6**

Peter also gives us excellent instructions and promises if we follow God's laws:

> **For if these things be in you, and abound, they make you that ye shall neither be barren nor unfruitful in the knowledge of our Lord Jesus Christ.**
>
> **II Peter 1:8**

## The Bottom Line

I think I have found the bottom line in what God is looking for in the following passage of Scripture:

> **There is that scattereth, and yet increaseth; and there is that withholdeth more than is meet, but it tendeth to poverty.**
>
> **The liberal soul shall be made fat: and he that watereth shall be watered also himself.**
>
> **Proverbs 11:24-25**

First, God tantalized us with, "There is that scattereth, and yet increaseth...." Then He came right out and said in no unmistakable terms, **"The liberal soul shall be made fat."**

## Excess—More Than Enough

The word *fat* means "surplus." It means you have more than the minimum that you must have to exist. If you are fat, you could lose some of what you have and not be hurt. Can you pinch an inch? I mean on your waistline? If so, that is excess—more than enough.

God says, "The liberal **soul** shall be made fat." In other words, if you are a **liberal soul** God will bless you with excess!

## What Is a Liberal Soul?

Your soul is the man you are inside your body. It is the real you. It is the part of you that will either cause you to be a failure or a success. A liberal soul is something you **are** or **are not.** A liberal soul has a specific frame of mind to function in.

- A liberal deed is what you **do.**
- A liberal soul is what you **are.**

However, you can *do* a liberal deed and not necessarily *be* a liberal soul. You can be a liberal soul and not even be a Christian. And you can be a Christian and not necessarily be a liberal soul. It is the true **liberal** soul that **shall** be made fat.

> **For as he [man] thinketh in his heart, so is he.**
> **Proverbs 23:7**

Some people naturally have a liberal nature about them. Conversely, others want to hold onto everything they get. Let's look again at this passage in Proverbs.

> **There is that scattereth, and yet increaseth; and there is that withholdeth more than is meet, but it tendeth to poverty.**
> **The liberal soul shall be made fat: and he that watereth shall be watered also himself.**
> **Proverbs 11:24-25**

By using the term *poverty* here, the writer is referring to the opposite of *fat* in the next verse. When he says *fat,* he means *wealthy.* The scatterer (liberal soul) shall be made wealthy.

In other words, if you are liberal in your giving to others, you will become wealthy! This does not make sense to the natural mind. That's because this is a *super*natural law. The natural mind wants to hoard material things for himself, but the supernatural, **liberal** frame of mind is different.

## The Liberal Soul Mentality

What kind of mentality does it take to be considered a *liberal soul?* Isaiah 32:8 says, "...The liberal deviseth liberal things; and by liberal things shall he stand."

## God's Law of Bankruptcy

A study of Deuteronomy 15 will help you to understand better what God means by the term *liberal soul.*

> **At the end of every seven years thou shalt make a release.**
>
> **And this is the manner of the release: Every creditor that lendeth aught unto his neighbour shall release it; he shall not exact it of his neighbour, or of his brother; because it is called the Lord's release.**
>
> **Deuteronomy 15:1-2**

In the first two verses, you find that God gave His people a law to follow in the Promised Land. He called it the law of "release."

The Children of Israel were to set up their calendar so that every seven years all debtors were freed from their debts. They were forgiven of any balance owed, if they were of the covenant people (their brother or sister servant of God).

## The Measure of a Liberal Soul

Now, in order to determine whether or not you are a liberal soul, ask yourself this question: *In view of this law of release in the seventh year, would I be more inclined to loan to my poor brother in the first or in the sixth years?*

If your answer is, "In the first year with an increasing decline in desire toward the seventh year," then you need to work on your attitude. Let's see why.

Look at what God says:

> "...You shall open your hand wide to him [your brother] and willingly lend him sufficient for his need, whatever he needs.
>
> "*Beware lest there be a wicked thought in your heart,* saying, 'The seventh year, the year of release, is at hand,' and your eye be evil against your poor brother and you give him nothing...and it become sin among you.
>
> "You shall surely give to him, and *your heart should not be grieved* when you give to him, because *for this thing* the Lord your God will bless you in *all your works and in all to which you put your hand [to]."*
>
> **Deuteronomy 15:8-10 (NKJV)**

What a requirement!! But what a promise!! These verses show what kind of attitude God is looking for, and they certainly describe a liberal soul.

Yes, people sometimes take advantage of the liberal

soul, but God said HE would make it up. God will give you more than the devil can ever take. It is a matter of **trusting God as your source.** The liberal soul shall be made fat.

## The Liberal Versus Non-Liberal Soul

The liberal soul says, "Here, you want my coat, take my cloak also." The non-liberal soul says, "How about this old shirt, I was going to put in the rummage sale? I will give you that."

The liberal soul says, "You want me to go a mile? Why, I will go with you two miles." The non-liberal soul says, "How about if I walk you to the corner?"

The **liberal soul** shall be made fat.

The liberal soul says, "Praise God, it is offering time." The non-liberal soul says, "Well, I might have known they would get around to this."

The liberal soul says, "Praise God, two offerings in one service—a double opportunity to be a blessing and be blessed." The non-liberal soul says, "Two offerings in one church service! How much money does it take to run this place? Don't these people ever get enough?"

**The liberal soul shall be made fat.**

The liberal soul considers giving an **opportunity.** The non-liberal soul views it as an **obligation.**

The liberal soul gives **cheerfully.** The non-liberal soul gives **mournfully** and **grudgingly.**

The liberal soul gives **above and beyond** the call of duty. The non-liberal soul gives only **minimums,** his fair share.

The liberal soul is the strong supporting the weak. The non-liberal soul is the weak supported by the strong.

The liberal soul tithes on all his increase. The non-liberal soul tithes on his net, after taxes. (By the way, if you tithe on the net after taxes, then the government is getting your first-fruits and God is getting your second-fruits!)

The liberal soul rounds off his tithe check to the next highest figure. The non-liberal soul makes out his check to the penny, $21.99, making sure he keeps every penny of his money.

The **liberal soul** shall be made fat.

## Rejoice with Those Who Rejoice

The liberal soul rejoices at someone else's prosperity, "Rejoice with them that do rejoice" (Romans 12:15). I can hear the liberal soul now: "You got a new Cadillac? Wow! That's wonderful! I am so glad to hear it. You deserve it."

However, the non-liberal soul says, "You got a new what? Cadillac! How did you ever get that?" I can see him walk away, moaning, "God, why does everybody else get blessed but me? I work my fingers to the bone and it seems like everything I touch turns to mud."

The answer is...**the liberal soul shall be made fat.** If you are not a liberal soul, God says the blessings of excess will purposely avoid you.

The non-liberal soul is the one who resents and persecutes the prosperous. He does not rejoice with those who rejoice. Nor does he weep with those who weep. I can hear him as he receives news that his friend wrecked his new car: "Ha, he did not deserve it in the first place." The non-liberal soul rejoices over those who weep, and weeps over those who rejoice.

**The liberal soul shall be made fat.**

## Good Receivers

Another thing about the liberal soul is that he has no problem with being a good receiver. He knows that the more he receives, the more he can give, and giving is what pleases him most. He is not timid about receiving. He knows he cannot give more unless he has more to give.

Well, have you located yourself yet?

## The Red Dot

I was looking for a certain store in a huge shopping mall one day, when I found a map of the mall on an island pedestal. The first thing I did, after finding the map, was to pinpoint my present location which was marked by a big red dot. From there, I was able to locate the store and find my way to it.

Can you find your red dot?

I hope my description of the difference between a liberal and a non-liberal soul helps you find where you presently are, so you can get to where you want to go.

**The liberal soul shall be made fat.**

The liberal soul would rather be caught doing more than his fair share, than to withhold more than is appropriate.

The following poem is a fitting description of the difference between a liberal and a non-liberal soul. Read it and search yourself.

## The Key to Living Is Giving

A very favorite story of mine
Is about two seas in Palestine.

One is a sparkling sapphire jewel,
Its waters are clean, clear and cool.
Along its shores the children play
And travelers seek it on their way,
And Nature gives so lavishly
Her choicest gems to the Galilee:

But on to the south the Jordan flows
Into a sea where nothing grows,
No splash of fish, no singing bird,
No children's laughter is ever heard,
The air hangs heavy all around
And Nature shuns this barren ground:

Both seas receive the Jordan's flow,
The water is just the same, we know,
But one of those seas, like liquid sun,
Can warm the hearts of everyone,
While farther south the other sea
Is dead and dark and miserly—
It takes each drop the Jordan brings
And to each drop it fiercely clings,
It hoards and holds the Jordan's waves
Until like shackled, captured slaves
the fresh, clear Jordan turns to salt
And dies within the Dead Sea's vault:

But the Jordan flows on rapturously
As it enters and leaves the Galilee,
For every drop that the Jordan gives
Becomes a laughing wave that lives—
For the Galilee gives back each drop,
Its waters flow and never stop,
And in this laughing, living sea
That takes and gives so generously
We find the way to life and living
Is not in keeping, but in giving:

Yes, there are two Palestinian seas
And mankind is fashioned after these!
                                    Author Unknown

# My Personal Testimony

I raise Arabian horses for fun and enjoyment. Some time ago, I had a fine three-year-old gelding that I had decided to sell. He was appraised by a national judge at $5,000, and I needed the cash to clear up some deficits that had developed.

While I was preparing an ad to use in selling the gelding, I had a nudge in my spirit to give him to a preacher friend of mine who had voiced an interest in having a horse like that. However, because I needed the money, I hesitated for several days.

### A Confirmation

After a while my wife spoke up and said, "Why don't you give him as a seed?" to this preacher whom she called by name.

I promptly picked up the phone and called my friend. He and his wife came to our house and excitedly received the horse. Before they left, he asked what we wanted the Lord to do for us. We agreed that we wanted to get completely out of debt. The four of us joined hands and he prayed, decreeing that in one-and-one-half years we would be out of debt. Believe me, that really challenged our faith.

We have never begged people for money, and I was not going to start then. So I knew it would be a supernatural miracle.

## Blessings in Abundance

What happened the **following week** was astounding. Three years prior to this, my former home builder had sued me for $40,000, because I fired him for not doing his job properly. The bank which held the interim loan demanded I do this, or they would call in the loan.

For over two years I had been through depositions and pre-trial hearings, and at this point had spent many hundreds of dollars on attorney fees. The trial date was set for December 6th, but my attorney called me the last week in November, two days after I had given the horse away. He informed me that the lawsuit had cleared and I did not owe anything! The $40,000.00 threat was suddenly gone.

The next day, God delivered me of a $12,000 **actual debt** and $450 **per month** overhead. I also received a beautiful Ninety Eight Oldsmobile free and clear of debt.

Two days later, I received in the mail a check for $5,115 from our insurance company. Over one-and-one-half years ago, they had refused, based on a technicality, to pay a claim. Now suddenly they decided to pay!

## The Rest of the Story

Another miracle came exactly one-and-one-half years later, to the month, after the preacher had prayed in my living room. While I was preparing for some missionary work and concentrating on getting money together to buy Bibles to take with me to Russia, God sent my wife and me a large sum of money from several sources. This money was enough to completely clear us of all debt, except for our house. This was the one exception the preacher had made when he prayed.

These figures may not seem big to some, but awful big to others. However, it is not the amount that I want to emphasize, but the principle.

You must get into the habit of seeing giving as an opportunity, not an obligation.

# God's Dual Concern

God never tells you to give to the need of others without also considering *your* need. He is not concerned about them more than you.

Remember the story of Elijah and the widow woman who was about to eat her last meal and die (I Kings 17). In a later chapter, we will discuss this story in detail. However, at this point, it is important to note that God brought two needs together in order to supply both. Each acted in faith, and God supplied both of their needs. It always requires faith to be a liberal soul.

**The liberal soul shall be made fat.**

# Collecting Unpaid Debts

If someone has not paid you a debt owed to you and you

have developed a strained relationship over it, why not just release the debt? You probably will not get the money back anyway. If he or she is a covenant person (a brother or sister in Christ), you cannot sue scripturally.

> If then ye have judgments of things pertaining to this life....
>
> ...Is not a wise man among you?...that shall be able to judge between his brethren?
>
> But brother goeth to law with brother, and that before the unbelievers.
>
> Now therefore there is utterly a fault among you, because ye go to law one with another. Why do ye not rather take wrong? Why do ye not rather suffer yourselves to be defrauded?
>
> Nay, ye do wrong....
>
> I Corinthians 6:4-8

However, by releasing him or her, several things are accomplished:

- You can restore the friendship and ease the tension in your relationship.
- That person will admire and respect you more than himself or herself.
- **Pride may even cause that person to pay you back!**

However, even if this man or woman does not pay you back, **God will.**

You be the strong one supporting the weak. This is a desirable and respectable position.

That person may not be poor financially, but if he or she does not pay just debts when the ability to pay exists, that person is certainly in poverty of character.

God promises He will repay if you give to the poor.

**"The liberal soul shall be made fat:** and he that watereth shall be watered also himself."

# A Time of Testing

Everyone who determines to let his or her soul function with a liberal mentality will be put to the test at some time.

I had an occasion to be severely tested on this sometime ago.

A Christian business man offered to cover the cost on a very expensive car that he wanted to give me. This was to be his donation to our ministry. Personally, I never would have paid that much money for a car, but he assured me in writing with all the proper papers, that he would be responsible for the costs. However, my name would be involved in the financing.

When I checked out his integrity with his pastor, I was reassured. Well, he covered this cost for about six months, then suddenly chose to discontinue. I discussed it with him face-to-face, but to no avail. I had all the proper papers that could hold him to his agreement, but he would not take the car back and cancel our agreement, nor would he cover any more of the cost. I could have made him pay through the courts, but I knew Scripture.

As I wrestled with what to do, I remembered the attitude of the liberal soul. In faith, I took the attitude of the liberal soul. I sold the car to cover as much of the debt as possible and agreed to make monthly payments to the bank on the balance. This was several thousand dollars plus 11% interest.

**God Made It Easy**

God spoke to me, and promised to make this easy for me to do. He also did a work in my heart and took away the anger and resentment I was wrestling with.

I paid on that note until I cleared half of it. Then God dropped an idea in my mind to offer to pay half the balance if the bank would clear the note. At that time I had accumulated some cash. When I called the bank, **they agreed.**

That was only part of the miracle. When I made the final payment, the bank employee informed me that **they had not charged me any interest on the entire note.**

*Imagine that!*

Not too long after that God put me in the same type of car, a later year model with a more desirable body style and with no debt.

The liberal soul shall be made fat.

If you want "all things to work together for good" (Romans 8:28), you must maintain the liberal soul attitude. Keep God's favor, and He will even cover your mistakes.

# The Prophet's Challenge

In II Chronicles 25, King Amaziah of Judah was going to battle against Edom. He hired 100,000 soldiers from Israel to go to battle with him and paid them $528,000 for their help.

However, a prophet of God came to the king after he had made the deal. The prophet told him that God would not honor it. He informed the king that God's favor was not on the armies of Israel at that time. He further declared that if the king followed through with this contract, he would lose the battle. The pressure was powerful and intense.

> And Amaziah said to the man of God, But what shall
> we do for the hundred talents which I have given to the
> army of Israel? And the man of God answered, *The Lord is*
> *able to give thee much more than this.*
>
> **II Chronicles 25:9**

Think about this! Are you committed to obeying God even in preference to losing money, if necessary? Can you trust God to restore your loss?

# Summary

With God, money is not the issue. **Obedience** is. God can always give the money to someone He can trust to obey him.

Where do you stand? Will you obey God? Will you have a perfect heart toward Him? Will you be a liberal soul? If you will do this for God no matter what the circumstances look like, He will bless you with abundant excess...so much that you will not be able to contain it all!

# 5

# Giving with Receiving in Mind: Right or Wrong?

There is a reason for the controversy that exists on giving. Debate on this issue never seems to cease. If we as Christians disagree on a biblical issue, it is always a result of not having a clear view from the same direction.

I have learned that the reason Scripture often seems to contradict itself is because I do not have a divine revelation on it. The Scripture, when seen through the eyes of the Holy Spirit, never disagrees. **The Spirit and the Word always agree.** In this chapter, we will discover what the Spirit and the Word have to say on this issue: Is it right or wrong to give, expecting to receive something in return?

In Luke 6:30 Jesus said, "Give to every man that asketh of thee...." Again in verse 35 He said, "...Lend, hoping for nothing again...." or in other words give it to them and forget it.

However, in verse 38 Jesus said something that seems to reverse what He said previously, "Give, and it shall be given unto you...." How? "Good measure, pressed down, and shaken together, and RUNNING OVER, shall men give into your bosom." Then He set up a governing principle for us to determine exactly what level of receiving to expect. "For with the same measure that ye mete withal it shall be measured to you again."

Now, which way am I to think in order to honor the Lord and be right in my thinking? Am I to give according to Luke 6:35 and hope for nothing? Or am I to believe according to verse 38 and give in hope and faith that it will come back to me in abundance?

## Practice Both Teachings

Personally, I do not want to set aside either one in favor of the other. However, I have found out how to do both, and I want to pass it on to you.

Let us approach this problem from the position set forth in Luke 6:38, that when we give we can expect to receive.

## Stop and Read Luke 16:1-9

First, I want you to lay down this book and read Luke 16:1-9, the Parable of the Unjust Servant. Come on now— follow my instructions! Good!

Now that you have read those verses, I want you to consider several things. First, did it grip your curiosity when Jesus said, "...For the children of this world [non-Christians] are in their generation [talking about their dealings with money] wiser than the children of light [God's children]" (Luke 16:8)? Does this teaching by Jesus bother you? We will come back to it.

Notice to whom Jesus is directing this teaching: His disciples. These are the men who are going to be responsible for carrying on this supernatural ministry when He is gone. **They must learn how to finance their work.** So, Jesus tells them the story of the rich man and his evil steward. In the first verse He says, "...There was a certain rich man, which had a steward; and the same was accused unto him that he had wasted his goods."

## The Dilemma

The steward was in charge of the rich man's business, but he had been accused of embezzling his master's funds. The rich man put the steward on notice that he was going to lose his job unless he could show in the books that he was not guilty as accused.

The steward meditated on his plight and sought for an answer to his dilemma. He knew that he was guilty and would lose his job. The steward was worried about his future income, so he pondered the problem. Paraphrasing it, the steward realized, "I cannot dig ditches. That would never earn enough money to maintain my lifestyle. Besides, a shovel does not fit my hand. I could beg, but my pride would never let me do that."

## His Solution

Suddenly, in verse four, the steward had an idea of what to do, so he would have friends to help him after being fired. The following verses tell us what he did. The steward gave all the rich man's debtors a 20 to 50 percent discount off their existing bills. Why did he do this? **Self preservation!**

Do you think the steward was shocked when the rich man called him in, having heard what he had done, and complimented him? After all, **it was the rich man's money he had just given away, was it not?**

Notice in verse eight, that Jesus agreed with what the unjust steward had done, and with the rich man's compliment of that steward. Why did He do that? Consider the rich man's thoughts.

## How Did the Rich Man Think?

Ask yourself, *If I were the rich man, what would I do?* Most likely, your response is this: "Punish the steward for what he did."

It was a purely selfish thing to do. He took advantage of his time remaining as steward to give large discounts to his master's debtors. He did this so they would help him when he was relieved of his job. That sounds like a wrong thing to do. Why would Jesus agree with this? We will discuss this in a moment. First, let us examine the steward's motive in giving the discounts.

## Did He Give Expecting to Receive?

Did this steward give with receiving in mind? Without question, he gave with receiving in mind. Verse four very clearly states this. Solomon noted in Proverbs 19:6b, "Every man is a friend to him that giveth gifts." The steward believed this principle, so he did it **in faith for his future survival.**

The steward gave these discounts quickly, naturally assuming that his rich employer would disapprove. If the steward was fired following his action, all the debtors would assume that it was because he had given the discounts without his employer's consent. Therefore the steward would be credited with the discounts.

However, the rich man knew that if he did *not* fire the steward, all his debtors would assume that the steward was following his orders. Therefore, the rich man would get the credit for the discounts, so he surprised the steward by **complimenting him.**

If the debtors were going to appreciate the steward for the discounts, most certainly they would appreciate the rich man. Also, if the debtors thought it was something the rich man had ordered, **they would make new purchases from him later and he would recover his losses.** Additionally, they would tell their friends and he would gain **new business.**

On the other hand, if he had fired his employee, the steward would then go to work for a competitor, and he would swing all the debtors to purchase from the competitor. Thus the rich man would **have no chance to recover his losses** and would even **lose the present business he had.**

Jesus surprised His disciples by agreeing with the steward's procedure, stating, "...The children of this world are in their generation wiser than the children of light" (Luke 16:8).

# Where to Invest

The children of this world constantly invest for the purpose of gaining a financial profit. Even Christians do this with their natural investments.

In verse nine, Jesus told His disciples to do the same thing the unjust steward did in order to finance their ministry. Read it again. He was telling them (and us) to invest money **into people** having faith in the principle that it would come back.

Jesus said this would work better than making investments in commodities: "Lay not up for yourselves treasures upon earth [earthly goods], where moth and rust doth corrupt, and where thieves break through and steal: But **[rather] lay up for yourselves treasures in heaven [people's lives], where neither moth nor rust doth corrupt, and where thieves do not break through nor steal**" (Matthew 6:19-20).

There is no chance you will take a loss when you invest

in people, believing God that it will come back to you.

Jesus said, the people of this world are wiser, concerning investing money, than the children of light. If it is not wrong for them to invest with receiving in mind, **then it is not wrong for you, especially when you put it into people.**

## The Pharisees

Now, look at Luke 16:14. The Pharisees understood the meaning of this story and resented it, **because they were covetous and faithless.** They did not want to turn loose of their money in this fashion, because they had no written contract for its return.

Covetousness is a problem we all have to deal with. A preacher friend of mine was asked, "Are you still into that giving and receiving stuff?"

He replied, "Which one are you against?"

**Remember:** "...Without faith it is impossible to please him [God]..." (Hebrews 11:6). It takes faith for you to invest without a contract and believe it will come back to you.

Observe closely Luke 16:11, "If therefore ye have not been faithful in the unrighteous mammon [money], who will commit to your trust the true riches [spiritual authority and power]?" Obviously true riches is not the accumulation of great monetary revenue. However, Jesus is telling His disciples that if they are not able to function in faith with money, then they are not qualified for God's supernatural power.

Consider every leading, successful ministry you know. Do they move in spiritual authority and supernatural power? Now judge and see if they are also liberal souls who freely give to help others with money and other material things.

# A Parallel: God and Adam

Shift with me back to the first two verses of Luke 16.

> **And he said also unto his disciples, There was a certain rich man, which had a steward; and the same was accused unto him that he had wasted his goods.**
>
> **And he called him, and said unto him, How is it that I hear this of thee? give an account of thy** *stewardship;* **for thou mayest be no longer steward.**
>
> **Luke 16:1-2**

There is an interesting comparison in verse two with the terminology found in Genesis 3:8-13.

The unjust steward in Luke 16 was called into question about his stewardship activities by the rich man. In Genesis 3, Adam was called into question about his stewardship activities by God. Jesus was referring to this incident when He told His story in Luke 16. The rich man in His story was God and the steward was Adam who had been unfaithful in his stewardship activities. God, of course, is the owner of all the worlds in the universe except the earth. Adam through disobedience to God, turned the earth over to Satan who is now "the god of this world" (II Corinthians 4:4). Because of this Adam was put on probation, so to speak, until something could be done to reconcile the situation.

God immediately spoke of reconciliation, and He also told us how it would happen. Speaking to the serpent representing Satan, God said that Satan would bruise the heel of the seed of the woman (Jesus), but Jesus would bruise Satan's head (Genesis 3:15).

# The Good Idea

The steward in Luke 16 sought for a way to redeem himself but found none except for THE IDEA mentioned in verse four. In general, Adam was seeking for a way to resolve his situation, but he could not find an answer. However, there is another Adam—the Second and Last Adam—Jesus. He stepped into the position of sinful man and began to give away the rich man's (God's) goods.

The good idea Jesus used was to give gifts to men: sight to the blind, hearing to the deaf, life to the dead, hope to the hopeless, and money to the poor and needy. Jesus is a light to them who sit in darkness (John 8:12).

Did this gain Him friends? Absolutely! The poor heard Him gladly but all the credit went to God **(the rich man)** for Jesus called them the works of the Father.

Did the Father agree with what Jesus did?

He was commended of the Father when He was baptized by John in the river Jordan. A voice came out of Heaven, saying, "...This is my beloved Son, in whom I am well pleased" (Matthew 3:17).

By the way, did you notice to whom Jesus was giving the rich man's goods? The rich man's debtors!!

Right? Sinful man.

Remember what Jesus said to the Pharisees, "Search the scriptures; for...they are they which testify OF ME" (John 5:39).

# John 3:16

Now let us observe the Ultimate Gift of all time and see if we can learn some more about God's law of seedtime and harvest, sowing and reaping.

Under the first man, Adam, we were all brought under sin. But consider the golden text of the Bible, John 3:16, "For God so loved the world, that he gave his only begotten Son, that whosoever believeth in him should not perish, but have everlasting life."

God is obviously concerned about rectifying the wrong done by man. The word *love* is mentioned in this verse, and it was this love that motivated God to do something.

## God's Efforts to Restore Man

God had already done several things to restore man. He sent a flood to purge sin from the earth, but no sooner had the water subsided till Noah's son sinned again.

He let the people of Israel live in the squalor of poverty and servitude in Egypt for 400 years. Then He led them out by supernatural miracles. He also led them for 40 years in the wilderness, in an effort to teach and train them. However they only complained and sinned more. This angered God.

In another effort to bring them back into fellowship, He gave Moses the Ten Commandments to show man right from wrong. But they only revealed man's sin to him, and this made him all the more guilty.

Now man sinned intelligently.

Then God showed man how to sacrifice bulls and goats as a substitute for his own blood. But it was not possible for the blood of bulls and goats to totally remit man's sin.

Next God arranged judges for man. The judges punished sin, but this did not stop man from sinning. Man thought if he had a king that would resolve his problems, but the kings only taxed him and made his problems worse.

So God sent the prophets, but man stoned them and

killed them. This was followed by 400 years of no effort—the silent years. Obviously God was not passionately anticipating what He knew He had to do. "But when the fulness of the time was come, God sent forth his Son, made of a woman, made under the law" (Galatians 4:4).

## God's Motive

The word *love* mentioned in John 3:16 was God's motive. But nothing God did in love prior to Jesus resolved the problem and brought man back to Him. So He had to **change His method** and do a drastic thing.

## God's Method

He "gave" His only begotten Son.

*Love* was God's *motive* for what He did. *Giving* was His *method.* **All previous methods had failed.**

Let me ask you something. **Did God give Jesus to get us?** Did God give to get??

Absolutely. No one would deny that.

It is like God is saying to us, "When all else fails in your efforts to change from poverty to abundance, from lack to plenty, from unfulfillment to fulfillment; do what I did, give in faith and you will receive in kind what you sow."

God wanted man back in fellowship with Him. So He **put His Word in the form of what He wanted to receive,** a human being. Then He **sowed it** like a seed in the ground. God could have put His Word in a flower, bird, rocks, animals or whatever, but He already had those things. He wanted man.

No effort or device arranged by the devil could stop

God's law of seedtime and harvest from working.

On the third day, God's seed sprouted from the ground, came up right through the rock, over the soldiers and through Pilate's seal. Jesus came up with new life and a new body. He resurrected in full power and authority to reclaim man.

**Did He come up alone?**

**Oh, no!**

Graves burst open all over Jerusalem. Paradise gave up all human beings who had died in faith but were still separated from God.

God had sown His seed and now He was reaping His harvest. Today, 2,000 years later, God is still filling up planet Heaven from planet Earth because His seed sown is **still working for Him.** Meditate on this!

# Hoe Principle

There are two methods for obtaining money on this earth. One method I like to call the "hoe principle." It is the world's method. Like using a garden hoe, you reach out, dig in and pull it to you, saying: "Grab all the gusto you can. You are only going around once in this life. Reach out and get it before someone else does.

"It is a 'dog-eat-dog world.' You have to look out for Number One or nobody else will. Work long hours and take on an extra job, if you have to. Put a hoe in each hand. If that won't do it, put a hoe in your wife's hand, if you have one. After all you must have money in this world. None of us can make it without it.

"Cheat a little if you have to. Lie some if you have to. I love the Good Book, Lord, and I want to hear it preached on Sunday, but this is Monday. A man has to do what a man has to do."

This describes the world we live in.

"Save all you can save. Spend only what you must. Do not leave anything on the table. One of these days, you will have a nest egg. When you have worked hard all your life and are now too old to keep pulling in the hoe, pull it up under you and sit on it.

"One more thing. Insure it so you will not lose it, and dare anybody to touch it." But suddenly you die and your heirs spend it in a way you would not have spent it.

We are all very well acquainted with this system, much of which violates the Christian conscience. You cannot steal; you cannot lie. Instead, you are to "give preference to one another in honor" (Romans 12:10, NASB).

This means that you cannot abuse your privileges or take advantage of one another's trust. But the question lingers, "If you are not a tiger, if you are not aggressive, if you do not drive and push in this world, how do you expect to ever get anywhere?"

## The Shovel Principle

Now, let us look at the other system—**God's method.** I like to call it the "shovel principle." You know how a shovel works. You dig in and pitch it out. Dig in and pitch it out. Dig in and pitch it out.

> There is that scattereth, and yet increaseth; and there is that withholdeth more than is meet, but it tendeth to poverty.
>
> The liberal soul shall be made fat: and he that watereth shall be watered also himself.
>
> **Proverbs 11:24-25**

Honour the Lord with thy substance, and with the firstfruits of all thine increase:

So shall thy barns be filled with plenty, and thy presses shall burst out with new wine.

Proverbs 3:9-10


Bring ye all the tithes into the storehouse, that there may be meat in mine house, and prove me now herewith, saith the Lord of hosts, if I will not open you the windows of heaven, and pour you out a blessing, that there shall not be room enough to receive it.

And I will rebuke the devourer for your sakes, and he shall not destroy the fruits of your ground; neither shall your vine cast her fruit before the time in the field, saith the Lord of hosts.

And all nations shall call you blessed: for ye shall be a delightsome land, saith the Lord of hosts.

Malachi 3:10-12


## Dig in and pitch it out!

Give, and it shall be given unto you; good measure, pressed down, and shaken together, and running over, shall men give into your bosom. For with the same measure that ye mete withal it shall be measured to you again.

Luke 6:38


Nothing about the shovel principle ever violates the Christian conscience. To do this always requires faith which **always pleases God.**


But this I say, He which soweth sparingly shall reap also sparingly; and he which soweth bountifully shall reap

**also bountifully.**

> **Every man according as he purposeth in his heart, so let him give; not grudgingly, or of necessity: for God loveth a cheerful giver.**
> **II Corinthians 9:6-7**

How do you purpose to receive? So give!

> **Give a portion to seven, and also to eight; for thou knowest not what evil shall be upon the earth.**
> **Ecclesiastes 11:2**

This is what the unjust steward did to preserve his prosperity in the future.

> **In the morning sow thy seed, and in the evening withhold not thine hand: for thou knowest not whether shall prosper, either this or that, or whether they both shall be alike good.**
> **Ecclesiastes 11:6**

Do not look for a quitting place. Keep looking for more opportunities to sow.

A newspaper reporter once asked H.L. Hunt how much money he spent annually on advertising.

He answered, "Two-million dollars."

The reporter asked how much of that did him any good.

Mr. Hunt replied, "About half."

The reporter then asked, "Why not cut out the half that does not help?"

He responded, "I would, but I do not know which half that is."

Remember: God is not a slot machine. You do not put in

a quarter, roll three lemons and come up instantly rich. **It is a system, a lifestyle.**

Sow in faith. Later, you can look back and see how much your situation has changed. Sometimes God's blessings are so gentle you might overlook them. Consider a letter of testimony I received from one of our partners.

September 10, 1990

Dear Brother Gerald Davis:

In 1987 you preached four sermons on prosperity at Lakewood Church in Houston, Texas. At that time we were $50,000 in debt and in trouble. Our jobs were very uncertain and our future did not look good.

However, we bought the tapes of those four sermons and began to listen and listen and listen to them. The message became a way of life for us, and the Word began to be performed in our lives.

Today, we have paid all but $7,000 off on that debt, have over $1,200 a month free from debt and have increased our giving to exactly $1,000 a month to God's Work.

In May of 1988 it looked like we were both going to be out of a job; **but** God [intervened]!!! In the last two years the situation has been turned around and now we are both very secure and receiving the favor of man.

Just last Friday my wife received her paycheck with a 9.8% increase in salary; even though they had stated repeatedly it **will not happen.** Over the last two years we have received over $10,000 in pay increases.

One last thing. God's ways are very strange at times. He began to bless us in the strangest ways. For instance our electrical bill dropped by $40/month, our vehicles' gas mileage increased, when we needed carpet He gave us $35/yard carpet for less than half price and when one of our vehicles would "act up" He would show me the cause and how to repair it at a fraction of the cost that a shop would charge.

His means of blessings were so gentle that many times we almost missed them **but** He is faithful to "perform His Word."

Thanks so very much for obeying God and preaching those sermons. Without them we would still be in bondage instead of rejoicing in the blessing of prosperity.

Yours in Christ,

Mr. and Mrs. M.P.

This letter was given to me three years after they purchased the tapes. Look what God did with their seed in only three years!

## Summary

Now in consideration of all these convincing statements, Scriptures and Truths that are so emphatic and obvious, how do we deal with Jesus' teaching about giving and lending with the attitude of expecting nothing in return?

Since Jesus does not contradict Himself and is certainly not confused, it can only mean that when you give to Joe, Bob, Sue or whomever, you need to get your eyes off of them for your return and look to God.

> **And whatsoever ye do, do it heartily, as to the Lord, and not unto men.**
>
> **Colossians 3:23**

When you give to people's needs, God considers it a loan to Him, and He plans to repay it!

> **He that hath pity upon the poor lendeth unto the Lord; and that which he hath given will he pay him again.**
>
> **Proverbs 19:17**

Look only to God for your return, and He will cause it to come back to you through men. God promised in Proverbs, "He that giveth unto the poor [to people in need] *shall not lack...*" (Proverbs 28:27).

We desperately need to reevaluate our thinking patterns. We must remember the sowing and reaping principle in everything we do—including our giving.

We smile so people will smile at us. We put out our hands so people will shake them. We show ourselves friendly in order to have friends. But when it comes to money, we throw down the shovel and grab up the hoe. "...Let him that readeth understand..." (Mark 13:14).

God sowed His seed expecting a harvest. Apparently He did believe in giving with receiving in mind.

# 6

# Windows in Heaven and a Cup Running Over
# (Personal Testimony)

In my 39 years of ministry, I have heard continually, "Brother Davis, I have paid my tithes and given offerings all my life. I have never had windows opened up and blessings poured out until I had no room to receive them."

I had no answer. I had not experienced that, and yet I had paid tithes all my life.

You are going to find this to be an interesting chapter!

While I was sitting in my office in 1978, I came straight out with God. I was not angry, but I was frustrated.

## My Frustration

I have always had enough money to keep my credit good, drive a decent automobile and live in a clean and commodious house, but I have never had surplus.

I told God, "You have called me and anointed me, and I have been faithful to the call and consistent in the ministry ever since. But I cannot do what You have commanded me in Your Word, 'Go into all the world and preach the gospel,' because I don't have the money. I just do not seem to know how to get it together."

I said, "Lord, You know how much money it takes to travel, buy television and radio time, print books and do all those things necessary to reach people."

Then I continued, "I do not understand, because I know You could give it to me if You wanted to. You know I would use it for the ministry if I had it. I know You have got it. Please tell me: What is the problem?"

I sat there quietly in a state of spiritual depression, but I was serious and searching. Deep in my spirit I heard God ask me a question. "I saved your soul. Did you do anything to get saved?"

I answered, "Yes, I obeyed Romans 10:9. I confessed with my mouth the Lord Jesus and believed in my heart that You raised Him from the dead."

I heard God say, "Good, you did what I told you to do then I did what I promised and saved you."

Then He asked me another question, "I have healed you numbers of times in your life. Did you do anything to get healed?"

I answered, "Yes I resisted the devil, and he fled from me. At other times I called for the elders of the church; they anointed me with oil and prayed the 'prayer of faith.' Then You raised me up."

Again, I heard Him say, "Good, you did what I told you to, and I did what I promised I would do."

Then came this: "Why are you praying for money? If you do what I told you to do, you will have it." Immediately Luke 6:38 came before my mind, "Give, and it shall be given unto you; good measure, pressed down, and shaken together, and running over, shall men give into your bosom.

For with the same measure that ye mete withal it shall be measured to you again."

I immediately pointed out to God that I was a tither and had done it all my life.

## A Sudden Revelation

Here is what God said back to me: "Yes, all your life you have avoided being a God-robber. That was *My* money. You just did not steal it. What have you given out of *your* money?"

> Will a man rob God? Yet ye have robbed me. But ye say, Wherein have we robbed thee? In tithes and offerings.
> Malachi 3:8

For the first time in my life, I saw it! When you tithe, you are not giving anything. You simply are not taking what belongs to God. You do not have 90% of your money left after you tithe; you have 100% left. You have not given anything until you give out of *your* money. Therefore, only what you give out of your money is seed sown to your credit. It is the giving out of *your* money that creates the harvest.

Then I saw something else.

By tithing (not stealing God's money) **you are keeping the curse off yourself,** because you are not violating God's commandment on stealing in Malachi.

> Ye are cursed with a curse: for ye have robbed me, even this whole nation.
>
> Bring ye all the tithes into the storehouse, that there may be meat in mine house, and prove me now herewith,

saith the Lord of hosts, if I will not open you the windows of heaven, and pour you out a blessing, that there shall not be room enough to receive it.

And I will rebuke the devourer for your sakes, and he shall not destroy the fruits of your ground; neither shall your vine cast her fruit before the time in the field, saith the Lord of hosts.

And all nations shall call you blessed: for ye shall be a delightsome land, saith the Lord of hosts.

Malachi 3:9-12

There I sat dealing with what God had said to me. Suddenly I realized that it was time to either put up or shut up. A good friend of mine once said, "God is a good checker player. When it is your turn to move, He waits."

I made a decision that day. I made up my mind to "prove God." That is when I loosened up and began to move in giving out of my money. I started looking for places to give, and they became opportunities to me.

## Blessings Began to Overtake Me

Immediately following that decision, I went through a severe testing of my faith. But within a year my wife, Thelma, and I were able to make our first overseas missionary trip; we stayed 30 days. Also all my bills were paid a month in advance, plus all expenses for the trip.

On our first journey around the world, we scheduled ourselves to do seminars and overseas evangelism. Without a doubt, I had entered a different way of life!

At that time, my dream was to be able to live in a home that was not crowded next to other people's homes. So I paid a down payment on a lot in the country. This was in a wooded setting close to our oldest son and his family. It was a lightly populated subdivision with several more lots connected to it. I also claimed by faith the lot next to me. It was not for sale, nor was any of the rest of the land connected to me.

Shortly after I was there a "For Sale" sign went up on the lot I had claimed. I mentioned it in the church where I had been preaching and asked them to agree with me about the purchase of that lot. One month later a man called me on the phone and asked how much the lot was priced at. I told him and he sent a check to me for the entire amount!

At this time, we were giving out of our corporation as much into other ministries as we were taking in personal salary. We had become liberal souls.

In my spirit, I also claimed the lot on the corner that was attached to us, plus three more lots. Within a few years, as they came up for sale, we purchased them debt free.

In the first year we had purchased a 14 x 70 mobile home so we could get started living on the land. After one year our mobile home was clear of debt and remodeled inside and out. At the beginning of the third year we began to build our new Victorian home on the land, and fenced in the entire property in the fourth year. Everything was clear of debt as we went, except the house.

One of the main reasons I wanted to build in the country was because I loved horses. Three weeks after we fenced in the land, I got a phone call from a woman whom I had only met one time many months before.

I saw this woman at a wedding and congratulated her on her recent accomplishment. She had won the Region 9 Championship with her prize half-Arabian mare. This made her horse the number one mare in the states of Texas, Oklahoma, Arkansas, Louisiana and New Mexico. In a show covering all 50 states she was in the top 20 mares in the nation.

On the phone she asked me if I would be interested in owning a nice horse. I knew she owned Arabian horses, not any "soap-factory stuff." I informed her that I had just fenced in my land so I could have a horse. She invited Thelma and me out to her place to look at the horse she wanted to give us.

When we arrived, this woman brought out the most beautiful white mare I think I had ever laid eyes on, at least up close. She was 16 hands high, man size, with a long flowing mane, and a tail that touched the ground. She was immaculately groomed, as was their entire home, barn and grounds.

The woman saddled the mare and showed me all the special training this horse had. She was thoroughly trained in dressage, English pleasure and Western pleasure. As I watched her ride, the woman explained that this was the horse she had won the championship with! I could see why.

She rode the horse up in front of me, dismounted, handed me the reins, smiled and said, "Here is your horse." My emotions went in every direction. I could not believe what was happening. She was giving me her prized champion horse!

Her husband looked at me and said he had been offered thousands of dollars (the figure was staggering) for that mare three weeks ago, and his wife would not let him sell her.

She said, "God told me to give the horse to Gerald Davis." God had given her two dreams back-to-back in which she saw me holding that mare in the show arena. She asked the Lord if He was trying to tell her something. At that point, she said God told her to give me that horse and He would do something for her that she had been asking for—

something that meant more to her than the horse did, although the horse was very valuable to her.

This woman said she cried for three days at the thought of giving up her mare. This had been her personal horse, and she had trained her for over five years. Finally, she asked the Lord to take the hurting out of her heart, and she said, "Something came over me. Suddenly I had no more pain in my spirit."

When we started to bring the horse home, the lady smiled from ear to ear and never once got watery eyes. I was amazed. It reminded me of Deuteronomy 28:8, "The Lord shall command the blessing upon thee in thy storehouses, and in all that thou settest thine hand unto; and he shall bless thee in the land which the Lord thy God giveth thee." I wish you could hear her testimony of the thing that she experienced after that.

As we stood there, looking at that animal, I realized that I did not even have a barn. I could not leave her out in the pasture under the rain and dew. I had to build a barn. I turned and mentioned it to the lady. She agreed to keep the horse there for two weeks until I could get my barn built.

As I pushed open the main gate for Thelma to drive the car through, the Lord spoke to me. His words will ring in my ears to the day I die. He said, "I told you that I would bless you till you did not have room to receive it" (Malachi 3:10). Well, I certainly did not have room to receive this prized horse; I had to build a place for her!

Never before in my life had I understood that verse. Now, suddenly I realized that God was simply saying that He would bless us in our businesses and personal lives by giving us increase, so we would have to expand our facilities and hire more help. We would also have to buy more equipment to be able to handle the increased production.

My cup was running over.

> Thou preparest a table before me in the presence of mine enemies: thou anointest my head with oil; my cup runneth over.
>
> **Psalm 23:5**

What does it mean to have your cup running over? Obviously, it means you need to expand your accommodations. I know God is not a waster. What happens to the excess when your cup runs over? *You should put a saucer under it, and use the excess to promote the Lord's work.* He gives you the "power to get wealth so you may establish HIS covenant" (Deuteronomy 8:18). The ungodly will not do it, and you cannot do it unless you have the surplus.

We had two foals out of that mare. One we gave away, (as told earlier in the book) and the other is a filly which we kept for foal bearing. Now God has blessed us with our own beautiful stallion.

Yes, I know it is true, "God always gives His best to those who leave the choice with Him." God is only limited by the limitations we place on him.

## Stopping the Devourer

Remember God's words in Malachi 3:11, **"And I will rebuke the devourer for your sakes...."** Who is responsible for your material losses? Here, God says that there is a devourer—someone who is trying to destroy whatever it is that God arranges for you to get.

In I Peter 5:8 we are commanded: "Be sober, [not drunk on ignorance and carelessness] be vigilant; because your adversary the devil, as a roaring lion, walketh about, seeking whom he may devour."

Obviously, Satan is the one God is referring to in Malachi 3:11. He walks around seeking whom he may devour. I am sure you have noticed that Satan takes advantage of every opportunity. But God said He would stop Satan's efforts and render him ineffective on your behalf. If you know this and will stand with God in a position of resistance, you can have God's miracle of deliverance from Satan's destructive efforts.

# A Diesel Engine

The following incident happened to me as a direct result of my claim on Malachi 3:11. I had just returned from crusades in Nigeria, Africa. I had paid another minister's round-trip expenses, but upon returning home I discovered I had no cash flow remaining. I needed a special divine supply immediately.

A Mercedes automobile with a diesel engine was made available for me to drive at no cost. The following Sunday I was preaching for a church in South Texas about one-and-a-half hours from my home. As I drove there in the Mercedes, I was believing that God was going to work for me that day.

However, when I arrived the pastor brought me into his office and began describing the financial need of the church. They desperately needed several thousand dollars to meet that need. I prayed with him about it.

During the worship service the Lord spoke to me, telling me to sign my check from them and put it toward their troubled situation. I could not believe what I was hearing, but I knew it was God.

At the close of the evening service, God again spoke in my spirit, telling me to raise the full amount of their need.

Considering the size of the crowd and the amount, I staggered at this thought, but I knew I had heard God's voice. Miraculously the entire amount came in, in less than 10 minutes! I gave them my check as I had felt instructed and started toward home.

Noticing that my tank was nearly empty, I pulled into a station and asked the attendant to fill it up.

"Unleaded?" he asked.

I replied, "Yes!"

I forgot that I was driving a diesel car, because I had only driven it a short time. If you know anything about a diesel engine you know not to do that. Gasoline is approximately 30 times hotter than diesel fuel. All diesel mechanics who have heard me tell this story have agreed that the engine of this car should have been completely ruined in just a few miles.

However, six miles from my house I stopped to make a turn, after having driven 90 miles, and suddenly noticed a severe knocking sound. The entire car began to shake, and I immediately shut off the engine and checked the oil, not realizing what I had done. When I tried to restart the car, it would not start. Instead it shook and knocked terribly. I locked up the car and called my wife to come after me. Then the next morning I called the auto dealership to send a wrecker for the car.

At 4:00 p.m. that afternoon my phone rang, and a man at the dealership asked, "Is this Mr. Davis?"

I told him I was Mr. Davis.

Then he asked, "Who put gasoline in this diesel car?"

I nearly fainted when I realized what I had done.

"What did it do to the car?" I asked.

"We don't know," he said. "We have drained the tank and the lines, and have cleaned out the injectors. But we will not try to start the car till tomorrow morning."

I asked, "What is gasoline supposed to do to the engine?"

"Ruin it," he snapped.

I begged, "You don't mean I may need to replace the engine do you?"

"Yes," he added. "Replace the engine."

I asked, "You won't know until tomorrow?"

"Tomorrow morning I will call you and let you know what has happened."

I asked one more question. "How much will it cost to replace the engine?"

"$5,000," he responded without hesitation.

As I hung up the phone, I immediately fell on my knees to God. Yes, tears filled my eyes as I realized what kind of strain I was suddenly up against. All kinds of fear came to me from many directions.

My wife, Thelma, bless her sweet precious heart, brought me back to reality. She stepped up behind the couch, laid her hand on my shoulder and said, "Darling, if God could save your soul, don't you think He can fix that engine?" That is what I needed to hear, and as I thought on it I agreed.

"Father," I prayed, "I have just returned from Nigeria, and according to my figures I am $500 ahead on tithes alone." That sounded like a lot of money at that time.

"I gave all my income yesterday to the church," I continued. "Now I am out of operating money, and this happens. I desperately need a miracle, so I am claiming Malachi 3:11 right now. You promised You would rebuke the devourer for my sake."

The reader might comment at this point, "Well, that was your fault. You put the gasoline in the car." And you are right, but then I am not saved because I do everything right.

It takes grace to cover my sins and mistakes. And thank God that grace is available, but it takes faith to activate that grace.

Well, I went to sleep with confidence.

The next morning the mechanic called at 10:00 a.m. "You can come and get your car, Mr. Davis," he said.

I asked, "What happened to the engine?"

"Nothing," he replied. "It is running fine."

I asked again, "There are no irregular noises or mechanical problems of any kind?"

"None," he answered.

I paused, "How do you explain that?" I finally asked.

"I cannot," he replied.

Then I asked, "Would you believe that this is a miracle?"

He chuckled, "That is the best word I can think of," to which he added, "you are one very lucky man."

I thought, *Yes, the more you obey God and trust His Word the "luckier" you get. (Of course, it is not luck, but faith and obedience that brings you miracles.)*

As I merrily picked up my keys and started out the door to go pick up that car, I heard God's voice come up again inside me, "The man told you that it would cost $5,000 to replace the engine. You said you were $500 ahead of Me on the tithe alone. I just caught up with you."

I shouted and halfway danced to the car. I drove that car for over one year after that and never had any mechanical trouble. It really is true, my friend. You can trust God Almighty. It does not take God long to rebuke the devil.

Jesus said, "I beheld Satan fall as lightning from Heaven" (Luke 10:18). We trust Jesus—Whom we have never seen— with our souls that we have never seen, to save us from a Hell that we have never seen, and take us to a Heaven that we have never seen. But we have trouble trusting Him with the tangible and material things that we do see. Be a liberal soul, and watch the exciting developments.

## Summary

God will honor the person who honors Him (I Samuel 2:30), and He will bless the person who blesses Him (Numbers 27:29). God is looking for an opportunity to prove Himself to you. **But you have to move when it is your turn.**

# 7

# Tares among the Good Seed

In Matthew 13, Jesus gave four seed-and-harvest parables in succession. Consider with me verse 33 in the last parable, "...The kingdom of heaven is like unto leaven, which a woman took, and hid in three measures of meal, till the whole was leavened" (Matthew 13:33). The woman applied the leaven to three measures which Jesus called *the whole.*

In Matthew 16:5-12, Jesus called the **doctrine** of the Pharisees *leaven.* This is what they **embraced** or **believed** from the Word of God. What you believe in is what you activate your faith for. So you could say that the woman mixed her faith in all three measures of meal (provision).

## What Are the Three Measures?

Now, what are the "three measures of meal"? They are the three areas of Heaven's supply or provision for our human needs. There are only three areas of human need—**spiritual, physical,** and **material.** All the needs of the human makeup fall into one of these three categories, represented by the three measures of meal.

Consider now John's comment in III John 2, "Beloved [the born-again child of God], I wish **above all things** that thou mayest **prosper** [materially] and be in **health** [physically], even as thy **soul** [spiritually] prospereth." This is God's total desire for His covenant-believing children. Did God make this provision available to you? Of course He did...in the person of Jesus Christ. Jesus came to meet your every human need.

- He shed His blood to save you **spiritually.**
- Jesus bore stripes on His back to heal you **physically.**
- He became poor that through His poverty you might have **material** supply (be rich).

However, if you fail to mix leaven, your faith, into any one of these three areas of provision, you will not be mixing faith into the "whole lump." Like yeast (leaven) that gives rise to the dough (the whole lump), your faith gives rise to or causes your provision to manifest.

Question: Is it possible to mix leaven into only one part of the lump and not all three?

The answer to this question is found in the first seed-sowing parable in Matthew 13.

> And he [Jesus] spake many things unto them in parables, saying, Behold, a sower went forth to sow;
>
> And when he sowed, some seeds fell by the way side, and the fowls came and devoured them up:
>
> Some fell upon stony places, where they had not much earth: and forthwith they sprung up, because they had no deepness of earth:
>
> And when the sun was up, they were scorched; and because they had no root, they withered away.
>
> And some fell among thorns; and the thorns sprung

up, and choked them:

> But other fell into good ground, and brought forth fruit, some an hundredfold, some sixtyfold, some thirtyfold.

> Who hath ears to hear, let him hear.

Matthew 13:3-9


This parable deals with Jesus sowing the Word into four different kinds of soil. The first three types of soil bore no production whatsoever, but the fourth type of soil called *GOOD GROUND* brought forth production on three different levels: **thirtyfold, sixtyfold and one hundredfold.** This you might say represents one-third of the seed's potential, two-thirds of the seed's potential and all of the seed's potential.

If it was good ground, why didn't ALL of it produce one hundred percent of its potential? Was the problem in the seed sown? No, it couldn't be, for the seed represents the Word, and "The words of the Lord are pure words..." (Psalm 12:6). It is promised not to return unto Him void (Isaiah 55:11).

## Is It God's Will?

Was it, then, not God's will that all the good ground bring forth one hundredfold? This couldn't be the correct assumption, for Jesus told His disciples in Mark:

> ...Verily I say unto you, There is *no man* that hath left house, or brethren, or sisters, or father, or mother, or wife, or children, or lands, for my sake, and the gospel's,

> But he shall receive *an hundredfold now in this time,* houses, and brethren, and sisters, and mothers, and children, and lands, with persecutions; and in the world to

97

**come eternal life.**

**Mark 10:29-30**

And again Jesus stated, "Herein is my Father glorified, that ye bear *much fruit*...and that your fruit should remain..." (John 15:8, 16). This complies with John 10:10, where Jesus taught us, "The thief does not come except to steal, and to kill, and to destroy. I have come that they may have life, and that they may have it more abundantly" (John 10:10, NKJV). It is not God's will for the thief to be allowed to steal, kill and destroy.

# Develop Your Faith

Why, then, if it was God's will for all the good ground to bring forth one hundredfold, did it not yield this much? Many times Jesus declared, "...According to your faith [so] be it unto you" (Matthew 9:29). Your harvest depends upon your faith.

Paul states in his writings that every man is given the measure of faith (Romans 12:3), and that faith is developed and strengthened by hearing the Word of God (Romans 10:17). What you hear taught the most is what you develop faith for. **Ever-increasing faith means ever-increasing fruit.**

Seed is actually sown into the soil of your heart for the salvation of your **spirit** when you first hear the message of salvation. The same is true concerning your PHYSICAL healing and health benefits, as well as your MATERIAL supply. When someone ministers the Word of God to you in each of these areas, that person is sowing seed.

Your harvest depends upon what you do with the Word you hear. Will you mix it with the WHOLE LUMP...all three areas? The word *salvation* is commonly known to be derived from the Greek word *sozo* meaning "salvation for the WHOLE MAN." God wants all three areas of your life blessed so you will have a one hundredfold harvest.

How do you receive it? Your spiritual supply is the most important. Develop your spiritual harvest first, then the other two areas accordingly. The spiritual is thirtyfold (one-third of your harvest); either the physical OR the material would be sixtyfold (two-thirds). All three areas— spiritual, physical, and material—make up one hundred- fold (one hundred percent of your seed's potential).

# Know the Difference between
# Jesus' Seed Sown and Our Seed Sown

Now in Matthew 13, Jesus is obviously talking about Himself as the *sower* and the Word of God through Himself as the *seed*.

Recall Mark 10:29-30. Here, Jesus is telling His disciples that He would bless them if they would put Him first in their lives. If the disciples would give up all their natural interests for Jesus and follow Him, He would bless them with a one hundredfold harvest "now in this time." The disciples obeyed. Jesus rewarded them by "leavening the whole lump" or by blessing all three areas of their lives...**spiritual, physical and material blessings.**

*Jesus' seed* into the lives of the disciples were the words He spoke. The *disciples' seed* was releasing their natural and material things to Him. Today, Jesus still speaks...He still sows the Word into the ground of people's hearts across the world. *Our seed* is the dedication of our lives to Him. Putting Him first. For this, *we (like the disciples) receive a harvest* of one hundredfold production. This is also the harvest Jesus receives from the seed He sows. *Jesus' harvest* is the production that you and I generate from the seed He sows into our lives. Some thirty, some sixty, and some one hundredfold. Let's make Him happy and glorify the Father by producing one hundredfold.

## Water Your Seed

The seed Jesus sows (the Word of God), must of course, be watered. Watered with what? The washing of the water of the Word, over and over and over (Ephesians 5:26). Plants need continued watering to grow and produce. If only the seed of salvation for your soul is watered, then only your spiritual man will grow in your relationship with God.

You need to water the seed **in all three areas of provision.** Jesus said, "But seek ye first the kingdom of God, and his righteousness; and all these things shall be added unto you" (Matthew 6:33). He knew there were needs other than the spiritual, or He would not have said, "all these things," nor would He have taken the stripes on His back that you might be healed. Neither would He have become poor that you, through His poverty, might be rich.

## Why Was Production Limited?

We have established here that the seed sown in Jesus' parable was good and that the ground receiving it was good. We know that the seed must receive water, but were there other factors that caused the limited production of the thirtyfold and the sixtyfold? For the answer, let's go to Jesus' second seed-sowing parable in Matthew 13. Consider His meaning in this parable.

> ...The kingdom of heaven is likened unto a man which sowed good seed [the Gospel—Good News] in *his field* [good ground]:
>
> But while *men slept,* his enemy [the devil] came and sowed tares [bad seed—bad news] among the wheat, and went his way.
>
> But when the blade was sprung up, and brought forth fruit, then appeared the tares also.
>
> Matthew 13:24-26

Having a portion of **good seed** is not enough; we must also keep out the **bad seed.** Watch the seed that comes into your life.

Scripture states in Proverbs 23:7, "For as he thinketh in his heart, so is he...." You are the product of how you are taught.

- You can only **say** what you **think.**
- You can only **think** what you **know.**
- And you only **know** what you are **taught.**

You **are** what you **think** and you **do** what you **say.** If there is bad seed in you, you will produce undesirable and negative results. The mixture of negative seeds among the good seeds hinders your harvest. In other words, if you mix seeds of doubt, which create the negative, with seeds of faith, which create the positive, you will hinder the production level of the good seed (Gospel or Good News) in your life.

God warns in Deuteronomy 22:9, "Thou shalt not sow thy vineyard with divers seeds: lest the fruit of thy seed which thou hast sown, and the fruit of thy vineyard, be defiled." Watch out for bad seed. **You don't balance faith with doubt; you balance faith with knowledge.**

## Preach the Gospel—Good Seed

Now think about it. Jesus told His disciples to go out and preach the Gospel (Mark 16:15). What is the Gospel? As you know, the word *gospel* means "good news." What kind of Good News were they to preach?

- Good News to the **sinner!**
- Good News to the **sick!**
- Good News to the **poor!**

These are **the three areas of human need**...spiritual, physical and material.

**Good News to the sinner is that ALL can be saved, NO EXCEPTIONS.**

> The Lord is not slack concerning his promise...but is longsuffering...not willing that any should perish, but that all should come to repentance.
>
> **II Peter 3:9**

**Good News to the sick is that God will heal ALL, NO EXCEPTIONS.**

> ...As many as touched [Him] were made perfectly whole.
>
> **Matthew 14:36**

> ...And he healed them all.
>
> **Matthew 12:15**

Who his own self bare our sins in his own body on the tree, that we, being dead to sins, should live unto righteousness: by whose stripes ye were healed.

I Peter 2:24

### What then is the Good News to the poor?

Deuteronomy 8:18 says, "...The Lord thy God...is he that giveth thee power to get wealth...." **This is for ALL OF US, NO EXCEPTIONS.** To teach otherwise is to sow tares.

Regardless of a person's theology in this area, no one can deny that the Good News to a lost man is that he can be found. No one can deny that the Good News to a sick man is that he can be well. No one can deny that the Good News to a poor man is that he can be rich.

If you are being taught that it is not God's will for you to be saved, healed or to prosper, this obviously is bad news and not Good News. This is the sowing of **tares** instead of **good seed.** But, you say, what about the dangers that Scripture warns us about concerning riches? Read chapter 3 again in this book.

When I preach salvation for the lost, healing for the sick and prosperity to the poor I am preaching what Jesus told me to preach, the Gospel—Good News. However, if I preach Good News to sinners, that God will save them all, and then preach doubt to the sick about God's will to heal them all, I am sending forth both sweet and bitter water from the same fountain (James 3:11).

The same would apply if I told the poor that it was not **always** God's will for them to prosper. Under any title or heading you place these kind of words, with whatever explanation you use to qualify it, this kind of message is still bad news.

Good News in one area and bad news in another is bitter and sweet water coming from the same fountain.

James concludes by saying, "...My brethren, these things ought not so to be" (James 3:10).

If a person does not have entire revelation in an area, he should not dismiss it or be negative about it because he lacks the full knowledge to make a decision.

**Preach the Good News! Don't sow tares!** Jesus calls the person who sows seeds of doubt His enemy—**"...An enemy hath done this"** (Matthew 13:28).

Remember, Jesus warned, "But while men slept, his enemy came and sowed tares among the wheat [the good seed]..." (Matthew 13:25). "While men slept...." These people were not paying attention and were unaware of what was happening. You must be alert to what the enemy is attempting.

## Rightly Divide the Truth

In II Timothy, Paul speaks of "rightly dividing the word of truth" (II Timothy 2:15). He also speaks of Satan appearing as "an angel of light" (II Corinthians 11:14). Many times Satan uses Scripture to confuse the truth. This is illustrated by his quotation of Scripture when tempting Jesus in Luke 4. However, Jesus didn't set aside the Scriptures of promise; instead, He responded to Satan's reference to promises with Scriptures of principle. **You can never claim the *promise* if you are in violation of the *principle*.** (We will discuss this in further detail in a later chapter.)

Many students of Scripture have not learned to separate and align **principle** with **promise.** This is why there are so many different doctrines all derived from the same Bible. This is why there is so much confusion about the subject of prosperity. Many have simply opposed this message altogether, because of a **lack of understanding** and **balance of**

**comprehension** on this subject.

This would be the same in principle as refusing the message of salvation, because you feel it isn't fair for a JUST God to send a person to Hell who had never heard the Name of Jesus. You cannot set aside a scriptural truth just because it doesn't fit into your comprehension.

God has given the covenant person "...power to get wealth..." (Deuteronomy 8:18). Now let's understand that and believe for it.

# Summary

Remember, there are only three areas of human need— **spiritual, physical,** and **material.** These are the three areas of Heaven's supply or provision for your needs. However, it is **your** choice to believe God for your needs to be met in **all three areas** or for only a portion: thirtyfold (spiritual), sixtyfold (physical) or hundredfold (material).

Do you or a loved one need a spiritual blessing, physical healing or material supply? I encourage you to apply the seed-and-harvest principles set forth in Jesus' parables that we studied in this chapter. Stand in faith for your answer and believe for abundant results...and **nothing less.**

Keep in mind the foundational truth that Jesus wishes, **above all things,** for you to prosper in your area of need. As you believe for a miracle, mix the *good* leaven of your faith into the need you are believing for.

Then remember, what you sow in faith needs to be watered (by the washing of the Word of God) over and over and over again. **Liberal** and consistent watering keeps your *good* seed (that which Jesus has planted) strong and growing. Consequently, the bad seeds sown (such as lies, doubts and negative experiences planted by the enemy) will lose their strength and have to give up their place in your harvest field. As they die out, your yield—your answer—from the good seed will keep increasing in abundance! And that is our Lord's *total* desire for your life!!

# 8

# Six Hindrances
# to Receiving Your Harvest

Have you ever wanted to ask your pastor, "Preacher, why is it that I tithe and give but I have never had the abundance promised in Scripture?" Ecclesiastes 7:14 says, "In the day of prosperity be joyful, but in the day of **adversity consider....**" It is easy to rejoice in times of prosperity. However, when you are not experiencing abundance, you need to consider why. God wants you to prosper. What is hindering this blessing in your life when you are tithing and giving?

Several hindrances are mentioned in Scripture that inhibit and sometimes even stop your reaping process. In this chapter, you will discover several hindrances and how to overcome them.

First, I want to point out that it is very common for believers to tithe and give offerings, **yet fail to prosper.** In fact, this is the very reason that many people are discouraged from believing in the principle of sowing and reaping. While there are many Christians who can and do testify of God's blessings on their tithing and giving, there are those who do not see these blessings from their faithfulness in this area.

I have never heard this problem dealt with to any degree. However, Scripture reveals why several people gave or tithed in the Bible and were not blessed. Observe some of these examples with me. Maybe this will help you or someone you know.

## Winds That Hinder Sowing

First, before you can reap, you must sow. Make sure that you do not fail to give your tithes and offerings to the Lord. Ecclesiastes 11:4 states: "He that observeth the wind shall not sow; and he that regardeth the clouds shall not reap." If you are open to natural reasoning for not sowing (observing the wind), you will always find a reason not to give. Perhaps you or someone you know has said something similar to this:

- "There's not enough money to pay the bills."
- "They don't need it as badly as I do."
- "I don't think they really appreciate it."
- "I may need this tomorrow—no telling what might happen."
- "This giving thing is just a gimmick."

## Clouds That Hinder Reaping

If you overcome all the excuses for not sowing, and you give in faith anyway, then you will need to watch out for the other problem: clouds that hinder reaping. After you have sown, the enemy will try to present clouds of hindrances to prevent you from reaping your harvest. If you succumb to his tactics, you will find yourself making statements such as:

- "I don't have the proper education to be successful."
- "I am of the wrong ethnic group."
- "Nobody in my family has ever done much."
- "I live in the wrong neighborhood."
- "Nobody will give me a chance."
- "The economy is down."

Any of these thoughts or attitudes will cloud your faith and keep you from expecting to reap. God will not cut you short of your expectations. If you expect great things, great things will happen. However, if you expect nothing, you will not be disappointed when you get nothing. God gives you what you expect. Make sure you are *expecting* to reap your harvest.

# Examples of Tithing and Not Reaping Abundance

### The Pharisees
Jesus' castigating remarks to the Pharisees in Matthew 23:23 will teach you some very powerful truths which could change your life if you observe them.

> **Woe unto you, scribes and Pharisees [Notice that He did not say, "Bless you."]...for ye pay tithe of mint and anise and cummin, and have omitted the weightier matters of the law, *judgment, mercy, and faith:* these ought ye to have done, and not to leave the other undone.**
> **Matthew 23:23**

*Woe* does not mean blessing; rather, it is an exclamation of vehement disapproval. The scribes and Pharisees were tithers, but Jesus did not bless them or their tithes. Instead,

He pronounced woes on them. How could this be? What was their problem? Jesus explained that simply tithing is not enough. The scribes and Pharisees had failed to fulfill "the weightier matters of the law, judgment, mercy, and faith."

**Judgment.** This is one of the weightier matters that will hinder your reaping. Most people are inclined to judge others and justify themselves. However, if you judge others, Jesus said that judgment will come back on you (Matthew 7:1-5); and if you justify yourself you will be condemned (I Samuel 15:1-35).

What your carnal nature teaches you is backwards from what the Word teaches you. The Truth is this: You are to *judge yourself* and *justify others*. If you do this, you also will be justified. So, learn to judge yourself, if you want God's blessing on your tithing. This is not easy, but it is necessary.

**Mercy.** Another weightier matter is mercy. Here Jesus is telling us that if we are not merciful toward others, our tithing will not be blessed.

It is not hard to be merciful to others, if you think of how you would want to be treated in their situation. "Therefore, whatever you want men to do to you, do also to them, for this is the Law and the Prophets" (Matthew 7:12, NKJV). This is the golden rule of the Bible. **If you fail to do this, your tithing blessing will be interrupted.**

**Faith.** The last weightier matter found in Matthew 23:23 is faith. Remember, "...For whatsoever is not of faith is sin" (Romans 14:23). You must be sure to tithe in faith, because tithing without faith is only being religious. Think about that when you tithe. Thank God and **remind Him that you do believe.**

Realize that it is more blessed to give than to receive (Acts 20:35), because your giving is an investment. This way you can be cheerful when you give.

I want to restate this: When you tithe, make sure you are doing it in faith. Faith for what? God's promises: (1) **Blessings poured out** until you do not have room to receive them; **and** (2) for God to **rebuke the devourer** so he cannot steal your blessings (Malachi 3:10-11).

**The Drainage.** This first promise of blessing for the tither and giver deals with income. However, mere income is not enough. This is why the second promise, that the devourer be rebuked, deals directly with the problem of drainage. This, of course, is speaking of Satan's involvement in your finances.

It is not enough to have money coming in abundantly, if it is going into a "bag with holes," according to Haggai 1:6. That will not do you much good. People have told me:

- "I don't seem to have a problem earning good money. I just cannot seem to control the spending and the dispersing of my money."
- "It doesn't seem to matter how much I make. Somehow it never is enough."
- "I work my fingers to the bone, but it I cannot seem to get ahead."
- "Where does the money go?"
- "I don't understand it. The more I make, the more it takes."

How frustrating! In Ecclesiastes 5:11 Solomon said it this way, "When goods increase, they are increased that eat them...."

**The Easy Yoke.** Notice Jesus' promise in Matthew 11:28-30, "Come unto me, all ye that labour and are heavy laden, and I will give you rest. Take my yoke upon you, and learn of me....For **my yoke is easy and my burden is light."**

When you **learn His ways,** your frustrating situations will reverse. His yoke (your work requirements) becomes easy and His burden (His lifestyle) becomes light.

I have learned that you do not have to spend all your time working for money at a job you do not enjoy. Claim better for yourself. To me, true success is when you are making a good living doing what you love to do.

Now let's take a quick look at several more people in the Bible who gave and tithed but did not get blessed.

## Cain and Abel

In Genesis 4, Cain and his brother Abel each gave offerings to God. However, God blessed Abel's offering and refused Cain's. When Cain complained, God responded with this statement, "If thou doest well, shalt thou not be accepted?" (Genesis 4:7). **Obviously there was something else God was looking for along with Cain's offering.**

## Saul

King Saul gave offerings to God on the mountain while waiting for the Prophet Samuel. However, instead of being blessed for them, he lost his kingdom and his anointing. Saul received woe instead of blessings (I Samuel 13:1-14).

## Ananias and Sapphira

Ananias and Sapphira were struck dead after giving an offering in deceit (Acts 5:1-11). This certainly was not a blessing.

# Doing the Right Thing the Wrong Way

Each of these people in the Bible gave tithes or offerings to God. Outwardly to man, it may have looked like a good thing to do. Yet something was amiss. It is necessary to observe that you can do the *right thing* in the *wrong way* and so miss the promised blessing. What looks right to man may be foolishness to God.

## David's Pursuit of Prosperity

Ponder with me an occasion in II Samuel 6 when David took 30,000 soldiers to Gibeah to move the Ark of the Covenant from Saul's hometown to Jerusalem. This was David's right as the new king.

The Ark of the Covenant was the symbol of God's blessings on His people. Blessings and prosperity were given to those who embraced the laws written on the stones inside the Ark. But upon those who desired the blessing *without embracing the laws* within the Ark, it brought a curse. In I Samuel 5-6, the Philistines were struck with emerods (hemorrhoids) when they possessed the Ark, but did not embrace the laws within.

David respected the laws within, but **he was not careful in following God's instructions.** He had the Ark placed on a cart drawn by two oxen for the journey; but God's clear instructions (in the Book of Leviticus) stated that when moving the Ark, it was to be carried on poles between two priests.

When David and his people reached a certain place along the highway, the cart's wheel fell into a hole in the road. The Ark slipped from its place and hung precariously on the edge of the cart. When it looked like it was about to fall into the dirt, the priest Uzzah reached his hand up to steady the Ark. But when he touched it he fell dead.

To the natural mind it would seem commendable that the young priest cared enough about the Ark to try to protect it from falling into the dirt. No wonder Scripture warns, "There is a way that seemeth right unto a man, but the end thereof are the ways of death" (Proverbs 16:25). The end result also produces disappointment, discouragement, confusion, sickness, accidents, unnecessary trouble, poverty, want and lack.

This may seem like a technicality to us, but God had His reason for His requirements. Man's response is simply to obey. This disobedience caused the death of a priest and stopped the process of prosperity towards Jerusalem.

Later, after David checked the instructions and found his problem, he went to get the Ark a second time using God's way (I Chronicles 15). The reason David made a second effort was because he had heard how God was blessing the house of Obed-edom the Gittite (II Samuel 6:11-12). David had left the Ark in this man's house after the death of Uzzah during the first attempt to transfer the Ark. God made Obed-edom rich in three months because he embraced His laws and blessings. Nevertheless, when David made the proper adjustments, he was able to obtain the Ark with its blessings. **Remember, when all else fails—read the instructions.**

You see, David wanted prosperity and went after that blessing, but he was disappointed and confused at the outcome. He had gone after the right thing in the wrong way. Many people have read and embraced God's positive promises about prosperity. However, in their excitement and effort to grasp the promises, they are met with failure and disappointment. What is the problem? The problems vary.

Tithing and giving is the foundational principle for prosperity, but obviously this is not all God requires.

## Six Principles to Claim the Promise

There are six principles—in addition to obedience, judgment, mercy and faith—that you must embrace in order to claim the promise of prosperity after you have sown.

### 1. Create the Proper Husband and Wife Relationship

In Malachi 3 God ceased to bless the people's tithes and offerings before they quit tithing and giving. Notice their complaint in verse 14, "...What profit is it that we have kept his ordinance...?" referring to God's ordinance concerning tithes and offerings. They were tithing but not seeing the promised blessing. Instead of searching out the reason for not being blessed, they justified themselves in not tithing. That invoked a curse (released the devil on their money). In chapter two, God explains why He quit blessing their offerings.

> And this have ye done again, covering the altar of the Lord with tears, with weeping, and with crying out, insomuch that he regardeth not the offering *anymore*, or receiveth it with good will at your hand.
>
> **Malachi 2:13**

Notice the word *anymore*. This shows that God had been blessing their tithing, but He quit. So, in verse 14, the people asked, "Wherefore?" or why? God replied:

> ...Because the Lord hath been witness between thee and the wife of thy youth, against whom thou hast dealt

**treacherously: yet is she thy companion, and the wife of thy covenant.**

**Malachi 2:14**

**Keep Your Marriage Vows.** The Israelites had ceased to keep their marriage vows. They were not remaining faithful to their companions. Instead they were having extramarital affairs.

Remember, Jesus said that you could simply look on a woman with the desire of adultery on your mind, and you would be guilty of this sin (Matthew 5:28). According to these verses, if you are guilty of infidelity—either in your heart or physically—it will cost you God's blessings on your tithes and offerings. This is a very serious matter. You need to think about it.

**Maintain God's Favor.** If you have found a wife, the Scripture says that you have "obtained favor of the Lord" (Proverbs 8:35). But if you are not faithful to her, you will lose God's favor. The Word also tells us, "The king's wrath is as the roaring of a lion; but his favour is as dew upon the grass" (Proverbs 19:12). God's favour will make to grow what you sow, so let the wise man take heed.

Remember, Sir, God has made you to be the priest of your home. Paul, in writing to the Christians at Ephesus said, "Husbands love your wives, even as Christ also loved the church, and gave himself for it" (Ephesians 5:25). Far too few husbands exercise this attitude toward their wives. In I Peter 3, the Word teaches that if we do not honor our wives properly, it will hinder our prayers. If God won't honor your prayers when you mistreat your wife, why would he bless your money?

Initiate kindness and thoughtfulness, and be openly affectionate to her in front of the children. Let your children see you kissing and hugging, instead of hear you fighting and saying hateful things to each other. Many children do not grow up respecting God because they don't respect their parents.

**Be Consistent.** Living one way at home and then taking your children to church to be taught another way is too confusing. God says in Malachi 2:15, that He wants "a godly seed." But that will not happen if children observe hypocrisy in the home. Be careful, Sir, this could be costing you your return on your tithing and giving.

**Be Wise.** To the ladies, who are reading this book, hear what Solomon notes in Proverbs, "Every wise woman buildeth her house: but the foolish plucketh it down with her hands" (Proverbs 14:1). I am sure you have noticed that if your husband does not prosper, it is hard for you to prosper. Therefore, how should you conduct yourself in order to help bring God's blessings on your family's prosperity?

Let's start with the question: Does your husband look forward to, and enjoy with excitement, coming home to you? Or does he try to find any excuse he can to get away from you? First, measure your attitude and demeanor around and toward him. Remember, he is a man not an angel, so help him to want to treat you right. Stir up some romance in your marriage. Think of ways to attract his attention, and use your God-given talents to keep that romance alive. Work at it! Do not give up easily! Don't be careless about your marriage! Spend time on it! It is worth it!

God loves it when you love each other and hates it when you fight. When you love each other, everybody wins. **Even your billfold and purse.** That takes effort and discipline, but it sure does make for happiness.

My father was a preacher. While he was the pastor of a

117

church in California, a woman called needing counseling. She came for a morning appointment with both my father and mother. This woman explained that her husband, Jim, would not stay at home in the evenings. Instead, when he came home from work he would get his bowling ball and shoes and head for the bowling alley. This took place five nights a week she reported.

"If Jim does not stop this," she exclaimed, "I am going to leave him! I cannot stand it anymore. I have begged, I have threatened, I have cried, but to no avail. Pastor, I don't know what to do." She was in the church trio and also a beautiful woman.

My dad, who was a spiritual man but also practical, leaned across his desk and looked her right in the eyes. "Julia [a fictitious name]," he said, "I am going to tell you what to do, and I promise if you will do it Jim will not go bowling tonight."

Julia's eyes widened as she leaned back in her chair. Then dad continued, "When you leave my office, go by the hair dresser and get your hair done in Jim's favorite style. Go by the lingerie store and buy yourself a pretty new gown. Then go home and prepare Jim's favorite meal and dessert. Take the children to a sitter. Have everything ready when Jim walks in the door. Meet him at the door and say these words, 'Hello, Handsome. I have been thinking about you all day, and I could hardly wait till you got home.'

"Plant a big kiss on him. Take him by the hand and lead him to his favorite chair. Push him down in it. Tell him that you have fixed his favorite dinner and dessert. Explain that you also have a special surprise for him. Bring his meal to him on a serving tray, and sit down on the floor in front of him while he eats. Every time he looks at you, wink at him.

"While he is eating his dessert, dismiss yourself and tell

him you are going back to the bedroom to get his surprise. Put that gown on and go back in, push the tray aside and climb up in his lap. Give him one of those really special kisses." Then dad concluded, "Julia, if Jim gets up and goes bowling, don't call me. Call the mortician. He's dead!"

Julia came back the following Sunday, and grinning at my father she said, "Thanks, Pastor, I think I've broken Jim's habit."

Remember, it is well worth the special effort, and **it also gains God's favor on your finances.** This procedure may not fit everyone's lifestyle, but you can do something to keep romance alive in your marriage. Isn't it worth the effort?

## 2. Maintain Positive Attitudes and Words

In Malachi 3, the people ceased to tithe instead of finding out where the problem was. This brought a curse on them, and compounded their financial problems. It also caused a negative and bitter attitude to develop in them.

**Profit on Your Tithing.** They began to complain after this fashion, "...It is vain to serve God: and what profit is it that we have kept his ordinance, and that we have walked mournfully before the Lord of hosts? And now we call the proud happy; yea, they that work wickedness are set up; yea, they that tempt God are even delivered" (Malachi 3:14-15).

Paraphrasing that in our vernacular, the people said: "What increase have we seen from our tithing? We struggle to do right and it seems everybody gets ahead of us. Look at the ungodly in their new cars and homes. They don't tithe, and it seems that they do all right. If we did some of the things they do, we would get zapped. They do as they please and seem to get away with murder. I don't understand, God.

I guess this prosperity thing just is not really true. What is the use in trying?"

**Do Not Use Stout Words.** God calls this type of talk "stout words" in verse 13. In Malachi 2:17 He says, "Ye have wearied the Lord with your words...."

**Use Faith Words.** Do you see any faith in that kind of talk and thinking? Hebrews 11:6 says, "...Without faith it is impossible to please him [God]...." The Word also says, "...This is the victory that overcometh the world, even our faith" (I John 5:4). You must give your tithe in faith, then your words will be similar to this:

> Thank You, Father, for Your divine plan of sowing and reaping. I bring You Your Tithe and my offerings with thanksgiving. With faith in my heart, I cheerfully give it to support Your Work. Thank You, now, for supplying my needs according to Your riches in glory. I know You will cause to return to me, a blessing according to Luke 6:38.

**Maintain Praise until You See Your Blessing Come to Pass.** If not, your mouth will hinder your blessing and affect the return on your offering. *Think on this!*

## 3. Put God First

**Overcome the Dilemma.** In the days of the Prophet Haggai, the people were having serious financial and material disappointments.

Notice the wording in Haggai 1:6, "Ye have sown much, and **bring in little;** ye eat, but ye **have not enough;** ye drink, but ye are **not filled with drink;** ye clothe you, but **there is none warm;** and he that earneth wages **earneth wages to put it into a bag with holes."** What a discouraging description of daily living. Then in verse 9 Haggai adds, "Ye looked for much, and, lo, **it came to little...."**

I, too, have heard remarks as distressing as these. One person described it this way: "If my income does not begin to exceed my outgo, my upkeep is going to be my downfall."

If you are doing everything you know to do, and you only seem to get deeper in debt—nothing seems to help— then there is a very good chance that God is not involved in your financial affairs. Satan is stealing, killing and destroying (John 10:10).

What was the problem with the people Haggai was writing about? I found it in the latter part of verse 9, where God explained, "...Because of mine house that is waste, and ye run every man unto his own house."

**They did not have God's favor because they were seeing after their interest in their own houses,** and letting God's house "go to waste." In modern vernacular, God is saying: "You are taking care of your comforts and putting them before My work and purposes."

**Keep Everything in Due Order.** Jesus said it this way in Matthew 6:33, "...Seek ye first the kingdom of God, and his righteousness; and *all these things shall be added unto you.*" Simply put, **if you take care of God's work first,** then He will see to it that you are blessed.

Take a look at Haggai 1:4, "Is it time for you, O ye, to dwell in your ceiled houses, and this house lie waste?" He went on to say in verse 8, "Go up to the mountain, and bring wood, and build the house; and I will take pleasure in it, and I will be glorified, saith the Lord," meaning they would gain God's favor.

The natural question that arises here is: "If I cannot pay my bills now, how can I pay my tithe?" But God makes the promise to you that **if you put Him first He will prove**

**Himself to you** by supernaturally supplying for you. God said:

> Bring ye all the tithes into the storehouse, that there may be meat in mine house, and prove me now herewith, saith the Lord of hosts, if I will not open you the windows of heaven, and pour you out a blessing, that there shall not be room enough to receive it.
>
> Malachi 3:10

**Know How to Have a Financial Miracle.** I have been a tither all my life, often when I could not meet my other obligations. I have inevitably watched God supply my needs. **Until you do this, you will never know this kind of miracle.** The only way you get a miracle is to need one. Have faith in God. Begin to tithe, and continue no matter what happens.

I tithe before I ever figure my bills. I take out the tithe first. Then if I need a miracle, I have **no restraint in calling on God to prove himself.** I never know how God will do it. Yet, He never runs out of ways to keep His promises.

**Who Is First?** It is not difficult to determine who is first in your life. Just observe yourself and then "consider your ways" as God suggests in Haggai 1:5-7.

Who gets the first money out of your paycheck? The house note? Groceries? The car payment? **Or God?**

Whom do you call first when you need money? The bank? Your boss? Your brother? Your father? **Or God?**

Whom do you call first when you get sick? The doctor? The pharmacist? **Or God?**

To whom do you talk first when you need counsel? The psychiatrist? Your best friend? **Or God?**

Where do you go on the first day of the week? Boating? Golfing? Working in the yard? **Or to worship God?**

"Consider your ways." *You can get God's help when*

*you put Him first and obey His Word in due order.*

## 4. Abstain from Strife

Paul appealed to the Romans, "If it be possible, as much as lieth in you, live peaceably with all men" (Romans 12:18).

Jesus warns that the Father will not forgive your sins unless you abandon strife and forgive your brothers and sisters of their wrongs against you (Mark 11:25). But how does that affect your return on your tithes and offerings?

**God Is Concerned for the Donor.** Consider what Jesus meant when He said this:

> **Therefore if thou bring thy gift to the altar, and there rememberest that thy brother hath ought against thee;**
>
> **Leave there thy gift before the altar, and go thy way; first be reconciled to thy brother, and then come and offer thy gift.**
>
> **Matthew 5:23-24**

Whom is Jesus concerned about here? Is it the receiver of the gift? Obviously not. The gift received will do the same for the receiver regardless of what the giver does. God's concern is for the donor. If he has strife in his heart toward a brother when he offers his gift, then apparently the blessing that is connected with the gift will be hindered.

If God will refuse to *forgive you* when you are unwilling to forgive your brother (Matthew 6:14-15), then it is easy to understand that He will not bless *your offering* when the same situation exists. Unforgiveness is not worth it.

**Beware of Bitterness and Strife.** Bitterness is like acid. It does more harm to the vessel in which it is stored than the one onto which it is poured. For example, it is better to lose money in a situation with a brother, than to lose God's favor

123

and blessing on your tithing and giving. Paul advised that it would be **better to be defrauded than to enter into strife with a brother** (I Corinthians 6:7-8).

**Know How to Recover a Bad Debt.** One of the best ways to retrieve a bad debt from a brother or sister is to simply write them a letter of release. If they are not going to pay you anyway, what can you lose? If you release them by allowing them to keep the balance owed, God said He would bless you (Deuteronomy 15:9-11). However, if they are not among the brethren then this rule does not apply. Be sure to read all of Deuteronomy 15:1-3.

Take your loss if you must, but **get out of strife with your brethren.** It costs far too much. According to these Scriptures, if you release your debtors, "...God shall bless thee in all thy works, and in all that thou puttest thine hand unto" (Deuteronomy 15:10). The amount of money should not be the determining factor here. **Trusting in God** is most important!

## 5. Know the Difference between a Vow and Faith Giving

Sometimes faith giving is called "making a vow." But the truth is this: *Making a vow* and *faith giving* are not the same. They are two entirely different approaches. It is not possible to mix the two forms of giving and make a *faith vow* or a *vow of faith.*

It is very important that you know the difference between these two concepts. It seems that most people do not understand this. Many Christians are in confusion and Satan is taking advantage of them because they lack this knowledge. It pays to know the difference so you, too, will not function in confusion. God is not the author of confusion.

Most information concerning vowing comes from Ecclesiastes 5:1-6. The first verse says:

> **Keep thy foot when thou goest to the house of God, and be more ready to hear, than to give the sacrifice of fools: for they consider not that they do evil.**
> **Ecclesiastes 5:1**

The writer is referring to the making of a vow and not paying it when he speaks of the "sacrifice of fools." This is sinister and easy to overlook, but it can cause long-term financial loss and trouble. Now notice what verse two says:

> **Be not rash with thy mouth, and let not thine heart be hasty to utter any thing before God [speaking of making a promise to God]: for God is in heaven, and thou upon earth: therefore let thy words be few.**
> **Ecclesiastes 5:2**

You see, God is supreme and can always keep His promise. On the other hand, you as a human being are subject to fall short of your promise. Do you see a formation developing here?

**What Constitutes a Vow?** Evidently according to the terminology used in Ecclesiastes 5:2, the writer is speaking of making a deal with God, such as: "God, if You will do this for me, I promise to do this for You." God calls this the "sacrifice of fools."

Let me be more specific. A vow is approaching God with a promise, asking Him to move first: "God, if You will save my life and get me out of this crisis, I will serve You the rest of my life." Or, "God, if You will help me sell my land for this amount, I will give the money to my church." Let me explain how doing this can get you into trouble.

**A Vow Is Legal.** There is no sin in making a deal with God. In many of the Psalms David did it. Hannah did it when asking for a son (I Samuel 1:11). Paul the apostle made a vow when he shaved his head (Acts 18:18). Jacob, on his way to Laban's house, said these words at Bethel:

> ...If God will be with me, and will keep me in this way that I go...
>
> So that I come again to my father's house...
>
> ...this stone, which I have set for a pillar, shall be God's house: and of all that thou shalt give me I will surely give the tenth unto thee.
>
> **Genesis 28:20-22**

Jephthah made a vow when he promised to sacrifice the first living body that came to meet him through the doors of his house, if God would give him the victory over his enemy, Ammon (Judges 11:30-31). Little did he anticipate that his only daughter would be the first one to meet him on his return. He surely was expecting an animal. However, he understood the severity of not paying a vow, so he kept his promise. What a sad story.

You should notice that **God is asked to move first** in each of these references.

A vow might be difficult for you to fulfill. Nevertheless, it is a legal matter with God. If you fail to fulfill it, serious consequences await you.

**Know the Consequences of an Unpaid Vow.** You see, according to Ecclesiastes 5:4-6, an unpaid vow can cause financial loss. Scripture says:

> When thou vowest a vow unto God, defer not to pay it; for *he hath no pleasure in fools:* pay that which thou hast vowed.
>
> Better is it that thou shouldest not vow, than that thou shouldest vow and not pay.
>
> Ecclesiastes 5:4-5

In other words, it would be better to do without what you are asking God for, than to have Him do it and you suffer the damages from failing to follow through with your end of the deal.

Excuses will not be accepted. It will do no good to say, "Uh-oh, I made a mistake. Lord, help me out of this." This is clear in the sixth verse:

> Suffer not thy mouth to cause thy flesh to sin; neither say thou before the angel [your guardian angel], that it was an error: wherefore should God be angry at thy voice, and destroy *the work of thine hands* [your material goods]?
>
> Ecclesiastes 5:6

You could be tithing and giving but have an unfulfilled vow which leaves the door open to the devourer.

Here is how financial loss can occur.

There is a better way—a way of faith. Vowing is Old Covenant procedure. In the New Covenant, "...the just shall live by faith..." (Hebrews 10:38).

**It Does Not Require Faith to Make a Vow.** Remember, a VOW always *asks GOD to move first.* It works like this:

- "God, You move first and then trust me."

On the other hand, the FAITH life *requires YOU to move first*. It works like this:

- "God, I am going to move first and then trust You."

Can you see the difference? A vow is God extending you credit after He moves first.

Now, since God does His part first when you make a vow, that places a requirement on you to do your part. It does not take faith on your part to complete your vow. It only requires **discipline, determination** and **obedience** from you.

**Choose Grace over Mercy.** A vow functions under the canopy of mercy. If you make a vow, you can only rely on God's mercy. While "...his mercy endureth for ever" (Psalm 106:1), Scripture also states that God has mercy on whom He will have mercy (Romans 9:15). Remember from an earlier chapter: **mercy is unpredictable.** Mercy is activated by God's volition.

However, **grace is absolutely predictable,** because it is activated by faith. "...By grace are ye saved *through faith...*" (Ephesians 2:8). "Therefore it is *of faith,* **that it might be by grace...**" (Romans 4:16). "By whom also **we have access by faith** into this grace..." (Romans 5:2). Repeatedly Jesus said, "...According to your faith be it unto you" (Matthew 9:29).

As you grow from faith to faith, you will move from "grace to grace." That is, your faith will keep you rising in your level of grace living.

Live in faith and grow in grace.

**Determine to Live by Faith.** This way you are not exposed to the dangers of unfilled vows and having the work of your hands destroyed. Remember, "...Your adversary the devil, as a roaring lion, walketh about, seeking whom he may devour" (I Peter 5:8). Do not give him an open door.

**Vowing Is Not a Sin.** As I said earlier, making a vow to God is not sin. You can still do it today. However, now you know what you are doing. Remember, if your prayer involves a deal that requires *GOD to move first* it is a vow. If it requires *YOU to move first*, it is a faith approach.

**You Can Choose to Walk in the Old or New Covenant.** If you function in vowing, *you are operating in an Old Covenant procedure.* The reason I say this is because the New Covenant (Testament) says, "For therein is the righteousness of God revealed from faith to faith: as it is written, The just shall live by faith" (Romans 1:17).

You can still make a vow according to the Old Covenant, and God will honor it. However, this is the same in principle as relying on the law for your salvation. Can you **absolutely** be certain that you can keep the law? If, on the other hand, you move into Christ Who fulfilled the law, you are trusting Him to save you.

Why not **trust Him with your money the same way you do your soul?** Live by faith and thereby live in grace. Give to God first, and then trust God to give to you.

**Repent for Any Unpaid Vows.** If you have made a vow that you have not kept, repent and acknowledge the Law of Grace. Thank God that because you are under grace, He "...is faithful and just to forgive us our sins, and to cleanse us from all unrighteousness" (I John 1:9).

**The Consequences of Unpaid Faith Pledges Are Less.** An unfulfilled faith pledge does not carry the same severity as an unfulfilled vow. If you do not follow through on your faith pledge, it is because your faith level is lower than your commitment level. Your zeal was greater than your faith. Your faith just needs to be increased.

The "work of your hands" will not be destroyed because of an unfulfilled faith pledge. You simply will not receive the harvest you could have received if you had finished your commitment in faith.

However, **the door is open for the devourer to freely plunder your material goods,** if you have made a vow in the past but have not dealt with it, either by fulfilling it or by asking God's forgiveness.

Even if you are a tither and God is giving you a return blessing, the devil can steal it because of your unfulfilled vow. **Know the difference between a vow and a faith pledge.**

## 6. Follow up on Good Ideas

Before I leave this chapter on hindrances to reaping after you have sown your seed, I must mention one more important point.

**Good Ideas.** I am fully convinced that many times the harvest is missed **because of our failure to follow up on good ideas.** I believe that good ideas from God are one way He blesses us and gives us returns on our seed sowing. But if we fail to utilize or activate these good ideas **we will miss our return.**

The harvest is not always a sudden gust of unexpected money. Paul warned, "...that if any would not work, neither should he eat" (II Thessalonians 3:10). God promises "to bless all the work of thine hand" (Deuteronomy 28:12).

If you are a consistent giver, you should have a consistent flow of money and blessings. But **you cannot give and be blessed as a substitute for work.** "In all labour there is profit: but the talk of the lips tendeth only to penury" (Proverbs 14:23).

**Do Not Take Shortcuts.** "Wealth gotten by vanity shall

be diminished: but he that gathereth by labour shall increase" (Proverbs 13:11). "The thoughts of the diligent tend only to plenteousness; but of every one that is hasty only to want" (Proverbs 21:5). Getting it the shortcut way with divisive means and plans will not last and is not the answer. God honors diligent thought and work.

> **He becometh poor that dealeth with a slack hand: but the hand of the diligent maketh rich.**
>
> **Proverbs 10:4**

**Work Smart.** However, it is not just hard work that God blesses. You also need to work smart, and God helps you with that.

> **If any of you lack wisdom, let him ask of God, that giveth to all men liberally, and upbraideth not; and it shall be given him.**
>
> **James 1:5**

Ask God for wisdom, expect it to come and then apply this verse, "I wisdom dwell with prudence [good, balanced judgment], and find out knowledge of witty inventions" (Proverbs 8:12). *Now that is what we need.* Good ideas will provide supply for your existing need. Then you must work *hard* and *smart.*

## Three Mental Virtues

Notice the three mental virtues offered as gifts of God, in the following verses.

> Through *wisdom* is an house builded; and by *under-standing* it is established:
>
> And by *knowledge* shall the chambers be filled with all precious and pleasant riches.
>
> Proverbs 24:3-4

Paul, in praying for the Ephesian Christians, said the following:

> Wherefore I also, after I heard of your faith in the Lord Jesus, and love unto all the saints,
>
> Cease not to give thanks for you, making mention of you in my prayers;
>
> That the God of our Lord Jesus Christ, the Father of glory, may give unto you the spirit of *wisdom* and revelation in the *knowledge* of him:
>
> The eyes of your *understanding* being enlightened; that ye may know....
>
> Ephesians 1:15-18

## Wisdom

Wisdom, a gift of God—which He liberally gives when you ask for it in faith—will cause you to get started in building your dreams. It will also help you to know God and His ways.

## Understanding

Understanding is also a mental gift. Understanding will establish your dreams and enlighten you.

Solomon said in Proverbs 16:22, **"Understanding** is a wellspring of life unto him that hath it...." And again, "...Therefore get wisdom: and with all thy getting get **understanding"** (Proverbs 4:7), and, "...Attend to know un-

132

derstanding" (Proverbs 4:1).

## Knowledge

Knowledge fills the house with riches, according to Proverbs 24:4. But understanding must come *before* knowledge.

Why is so much emphasis placed on understanding? Because of what Solomon teaches in Proverbs 14:6, **"...Knowledge** *is easy unto him that understandeth.* "Knowledge will fill your house with riches, but knowledge does not come until you get understanding first.

For example, you must first understand how math works and then you can come up with right answers. But be cautious here. Do not forget Proverbs 3:5, *"...Lean not unto thine **own** understanding.* "You need God to give you **His gift** of Understanding. Here is why: **"...The knowledge** of the holy [God] is **understanding"** (Proverbs 9:10).

It takes God-given revelational knowledge to obtain this kind of understanding. The wisdom of man is foolishness to God. "...The natural man receiveth not the things of the Spirit of God: for they are foolishness unto him: neither can he know them, because they are spiritually discerned" (I Corinthians 2:14).

# Summary

Pray for wisdom in faith. Believe you receive it. Ask for understanding. **Listen and watch for God's secrets to be revealed to you.** Then *work* on it. Have faith in the ideas you receive from God. If He gave them to you, you can make them work, and they will fill your house with riches.

If you are a liberal soul, the groundwork is set. Good ideas will come from God, as well as your miracle supply for critical and immediate situations. As you work hard and smart, in time you will have it coming in on every wave (Ecclesiastes 2:24-26).

Now I admonish you to go back over this chapter slowly. Think about the six hindrances to reaping that I have mentioned and meditate on them. Remember, when all else fails, **read the instructions** (the Bible).

I leave this chapter with God's admonition to Joshua:

> **Only be thou strong and very courageous, that thou mayest observe to do according to all the law, which Moses my servant commanded thee: turn not from it to the right hand or to the left,** *that thou mayest prosper whithersoever thou goest.*
>
> **Joshua 1:7**

# 9

# What It Means to Be Dried out to the Devil

Above all other interests, God desires three kinds of blessings for His children. As we briefly discussed in an earlier chapter, God wants you to:

- Prosper (materially)
- Be in health (physically)
- And prosper in your soul (spiritually)

Proof of this is found in His Word, "Beloved, I wish above all things that thou mayest prosper and be in health, even as thy soul prospereth" (III John 2).

## Satanic Desire

God and His children share an enemy who strongly opposes anything that God wants.

- God wants you saved and in Heaven, but the devil wants you lost and in Hell.

- God wants you strong and well physically, but the enemy wants you weak and sick.
- God wants you rich materially, but the enemy wants you poor and broke.

To keep you defeated, Satan will try to steal your money, kill your body, destroy your relationship with God and cast your eternal soul into Hell. Remember, Jesus said, "The thief cometh not, but for to steal, and to kill, and to destroy: I am come that they might have life, and that they might have it more abundantly" (John 10:10).

- God wants to **bless** you. The devil wants to **curse** you.
- God wants to **encourage** you. The devil wants to **discourage** you.
- God wants to make you the **head.** The devil wants to make you the **tail.**
- God wants to make you **rich** so you can **lend.** The devil wants to make you **poor** so you have to **borrow.**

If God is **not having what He wants in your life, then the devil is getting what he wants.** You are the one who determines whether God has His way or the devil has his way. **How do you stop the devil from getting what he wants for your life?**

## Satanic Intimidation

I want to ask you a question that I heard God ask me in my spirit, "Do you know why the devil makes people sick and poor?"

Immediately I thought, "Well, he hates us."

Then God's voice came again in my spirit, "He does it in an effort to intimidate Jesus."

I meditated on that with a rapidly increasing pulse. Satan uses me and my body to intimidate the One I love more than anything or anyone else. I become an instrument of Satan to intimidate the Lord, unwittingly of course. It is done unknowingly because if more of us realized this, we would no doubt put up a harder battle to stop the devil.

I can stand the discomfort of sickness and the inconvenience of being broke better than I can tolerate knowing that Satan is using me to intimidate my Lord.

You must hate him who hates God with a perfect hatred. You must get sick and tired of being sick and tired, and get fed up with not being fed right. This you must do if for no other reason than for the sake of the Lord Jesus. He paid the awful price to save your soul. He bore those stripes on His back—those horrible stripes with "a cat of nine tails" that historians tell us peeled the flesh on His back to the bone until it lay in shredded strips down over His buttocks. This He did all for your and my healing!

> **For ye know the grace of our Lord Jesus Christ, that, though he was rich, yet for your sakes he became poor, that ye through his poverty might be rich.**
> **II Corinthians 8:9**

He endured all that suffering and lack to redeem you. But if you don't walk in that redemption, Satan uses it to intimidate Jesus. I know that is heavy, but I have accepted the challenge. You do with it what you can.

# No Condemnation

God doesn't condemn you for being poor or sick. So don't get into condemnation over your condition. I am not writing this book to condemn you but to help you. Let this chapter stir you to a new determination to rise up and soar where eagles fly.

You can cast your fate to the wind, and hope trouble doesn't come your way. Or you can educate yourself in the enemy's tactics, and take control of your life in the spirit realm. Remember what God said in Hosea, "My people are destroyed for lack of knowledge..." (Hosea 4:6). God is referring to His own covenant people here.

# Ignorance Means Defeat

It is folly to think that because you are saved spiritually, you are automatically protected and saved from physical and material destruction. These blessings are available to you, for sure, but are not automatic. The devil tries to trick you out of your rightful blessings. (This may be elementary, but please bear with me.)

Paul warned his fellow Christians, **"Lest Satan should get an advantage of us: for we are not ignorant of his devices"** (II Corinthians 2:11). In Proverbs 11:9 Solomon declares, "...Through **knowledge** shall the just be delivered." **The new birth** only makes you an heir to the benefits. Deliverance from suffering loss to Satan in this life comes from **gaining knowledge of his devices**...learning what authority you have over him and how to use it. Then you must discipline yourself to apply this knowledge and authority. Be determined to exercise your rights!

To be well advised (armed) about Satan's devices is to

become *dried out to the devil.* In other words, you become wise to his tactics and therefore are a *dry place* where the devil cannot linger.

## Dry Places

Jesus explained several very important points about Satan and his devices.

> **When the unclean spirit is gone out of a man, he walketh through *dry places,* seeking rest; and finding none, he saith, I will return unto my house whence I came out.**
>
> **And when he cometh, he findeth it swept and garnished.**
>
> **Then goeth he, and taketh to him seven other spirits more wicked than himself; and they enter in, and dwell there: and the last state of that man is worse than the first.**
> **Luke 11:24-26**

What are dry places?

Why couldn't Satan rest and reside or even do damage in these areas?

Why did he get discouraged and leave these places? Was the house h⌐ went back to a fertile area for his kind of activities? I will address each of these questions very carefully.

First, what are Satan's activities? As we studied earlier, John 10:10 gives us the answer. **Stealing...killing...destroying.**

Stealing, killing and destroying can only occur where people are ignorant of Satan's devices according to II Corinthians 2:11 and John 10:10. Therefore, people who are NOT ignorant of his devices are the dry places where Satan is prevented from entering. That's you...if you are not ignorant of his devices. Remember also the Bible says that you are destroyed for "lack of knowledge." Therefore, you are saved from destruction when you are filled with knowledge.

If Satan, after having been cast out, was able to go back into the man in Luke 11:24-26, then evidently that man was void of knowledge. His "house" was empty of the knowledge of Satan's devices, or the devil could not have come back in. The man's house was "swept and garnished" (forgiven of sin and cleansed of devils) but **empty of knowledge.** If it had been filled with knowledge, there would not have been room for this devil and seven other devils more wicked than himself to re-enter.

The Bible declares, "...He that is begotten of God keepeth himself, and that wicked one toucheth him not" (I John 5:18). I like to read it this way, "...He that is begotten of God **[and] keepeth himself...**[the] wicked one toucheth him not."

According to all corresponding Scriptures concerning protection from Satan, you have to **keep yourself** from Satan's destructive works. See Psalm 91:1, "He that dwelleth in the secret place of the most High shall abide under the shadow of the Almighty." *You* choose to dwell in the secret place. If you are dried out to the devil, you will suffer no stealing, killing or destroying.

God's will is clear, "I will rebuke the devourer for your sakes, and he shall not destroy..." (Malachi 3:11).

Always remember, Satan can destroy us when we lack the necessary knowledge of how to overcome his bondages. For example, in the book of Job, we see that Job's lack of knowledge caused him great losses.

> **Therefore my people are gone into captivity, because they have no knowledge: and their honourable men are famished, and their multitude dried up with thirst.**
> **Isaiah 5:13**

# Stay in Faith by Thinking Like God

Another thought that surfaces from Luke 11:24 is that Satan is not satisfied unless he is doing damage somewhere. Thus the warning:

> Be sober [serious], be vigilant [or diligent]; because your adversary the devil, as a roaring lion, walketh about, seeking whom he may devour.
>
> I Peter 5:8

Satan is restless. He is always searching for an opening, and a place of habitation after a stronger one makes him leave his abode (Luke 11:21-22). Satan **must find** an opening. He can't just go in anywhere he pleases and do his dirty work, sow his nasty seeds and make them grow. He is looking for good, fertile soil. If it is arid or dry, he gets discouraged and leaves. It encourages me to know that I am discouraging soil to the devil!

Remember, "through knowledge shall the just be delivered" (Proverbs 11:9). Since you need to be educated about your enemy in order to be free from his activities, I want to take time here to share with you important information about Satan and his methods or devices.

# Victory in Every Battle

Through this knowledge you are going to become arid territory, or dried out to the devil.

I want to encourage you by supporting this teaching with these facts about my own life.

In the past 15 years of my traveling ministry, which keeps me scheduled at least 48 out of 52 weeks per year, I have not, at this writing, missed one scheduled engagement because of sickness, accident or lack of funds. **There is a way to stay on top of the devil.** Even when I had a heart attack, on a Sunday night after church in January, 1981, I was healed in four days and dismissed from the hospital with a clean bill of health. I was back preaching the following Sunday with no more problems.

By the way, there is a scar on my heart from the incident. Satan made his effort, but it didn't work. Scripture warns us that Satan will attack, but we are promised the victory in **every battle.**

## Satan's Attacks

Both my wife, Thelma, and I were attacked physically on our first missionary trip in November of 1979. In Sri Lanka, Thelma became sick during the night, and by morning she was so weak that she couldn't get out of bed. We claimed God's promise, "...He shall bless thy bread, and thy water; and I will take sickness away from the midst of thee" (Exodus 23:25).

We prayed and quoted the promise. I took her by the hand and helped her get up. She couldn't walk. I mostly carried her to the shower, stood her up and turned on the water. She stood alone, and began to bathe. We left on schedule that morning, and she was sick no more.

## The Holy Ghost Battles for Us

On that same trip, I spoke for four hours one day in the heat under a ceiling fan—no air conditioner. I called for a glass of water as I spoke, and they brought refreshing, cold water to me. After the meeting, however, I learned that the water I drank had never been boiled. We had tried to avoid that. The water had *amoebas* (microscopic organisms) in it.

Sure enough, that night as I slept, my temperature rose and I became extremely sick. I was so tired that I couldn't wake up enough to fight it with prayer. However, the most marvelous thing happened. While I was asleep physically, my spirit man prayed in a heavenly language. When I awoke the next morning, my bed was wet from perspiration, and the fever was gone. My body was weak, but I was not sick. I then remembered the battle in prayer during the night. It was very real, as though I had been awake. But I did not actually wake up. I remembered the teaching of Paul from the Scripture:

> Likewise the Spirit also helpeth our infirmities: for we know not what we should pray for as we ought: but the Spirit itself [Himself] maketh intercession for us with groanings which cannot be uttered.
>
> **Romans 8:26**

I had never applied this truth in a situation like that. You see, when we walk in the Spirit, Satan can never win.

> If we live in the Spirit, let us also walk in the Spirit.
>
> **Galatians 5:25**

# Satan's Methods and Devices

## Device #1: A Roaring Lion

> Be sober, be vigilant; because your adversary the devil, as a roaring lion, walketh about, seeking whom he may devour.
>
> **I Peter 5:8**

143

**Fear or Faith.** What would be your first emotion if you were walking down a jungle path, and suddenly you heard a lion roar not far from you?

Yes, I know, **fear!**

Satan cannot master you and do his damage until you believe for it. Therefore, he seeks to create fear in you.

For example, Job's hedge of protection against Satan was in his close relationship with God. However, when he abandoned faith and began to fear, the losses came (Job 3:25-26).

Remember, Jesus taught, "...According to your faith be it unto you" (Matthew 9:29).

Fear is believing. Faith is also believing.

- Faith believes for good things.
- Fear believes for bad things.
- Without faith you cannot please God; because God cannot do good things for you in the absence of it.
- Without fear you cannot please the devil; because he cannot do bad things to you in the absence of it.

Since all good things come from God, faith believes God.

Since Satan is the author of bad things, fear is believing the devil.

Faith and fear are both believers. One believes for good, while the other believes for bad. Whatever you believe for determines what comes to you. **Faith believes for the non-apparent. Fear believes for the apparent.**

- Fear judges by what it sees, smells, feels, hears or tastes.
- Fear is based on the natural mentality.

- Fear judges by appearances.
- Faith is based on the supernatural.
- Faith judges by those things which appear not.

The area referred to as the *real world* or *the natural* is always subject to the heavenly or unseen world.

In many of the Psalms, David tells you not to fear. Solomon warns in Proverbs 3:25, "Be not afraid of sudden fear...." In other words, "Don't panic!"

Pray and expect a miracle. God is not dead! He is watching you. He will never leave you nor forsake you (Hebrews 13:5). In short, when the lion roars (Satan), roar back at him with faith in God's Word.

**Don't fear.** When you do, you throw the door wide open to Satan! **Remember that!** Faith opens the door to God!!

## Device #2: Self-Condemnation

> There is therefore now no condemnation to them which are in Christ Jesus, who walk not after the flesh, but after the Spirit.
>
> **Romans 8:1**

One of the very best tools and devices of Satan is to put you under condemnation when you determine to walk in faith. It is one of his most effective tools. When Satan is using this tool, you will hear something like this inside you, "What have you done to deserve a miracle from God?" Or, "You have been too bad of a person to expect God to do a miracle for you." Or, "You are a black sheep; this will never work for you." Or, "You are just a born loser." All these negative, doubt-filled thoughts are lies of the devil. If you believe him instead of God, **you will have what the devil says.**

**Satan Is a Loser.** God's Word says that He has made you worthy to be a partaker of His divine nature (II Peter 1:4). When God forgives you of your sins, you are called "the **righteousness of God** in Christ Jesus" (II Corinthians 5:21).

> For God sent not his Son into the world to condemn the world; but that the world through him might be saved. He that believeth on him is not condemned....
>
> John 3:17-18

> Beloved, if our heart condemn us not, then have we confidence toward God.
>
> I John 3:21

You can see why Satan loves to use condemnation on you. He knows that your faith (confidence) in God will not work if you are condemning yourself.

If the devil wants to talk to you about being a loser, remind him of who he is. He is the biggest loser of all times.

God has forgiven you and has forgotten your sins.

Satan will never be forgiven or saved.

That puts you in the winners' circle. If God calls you worthy, then humble yourself and agree with Him. He is smarter than you are.

Accept His assessment of you, and receive His grace.

Put down condemnation by remembering that you have been forgiven of **all** your sins. You are worthy in Christ.

Now reach up and take God's wonderful grace. That's what this is all about.

# Device #3: An Angel of Light

> But though we, or an angel from heaven, preach any
> other gospel unto you than that which we have preached
> unto you, let him be accursed.
>
> Galatians 1:8

**Satan Comes Equipped with Scripture.** How does
Satan come as an *angel of light?* Here is how! He comes
through the mouths of men quoting Scripture. Or he simply
brings Scripture to your attention that will help you will-
fully sin. If you are looking for a scriptural way to violate
your conscience, he will help you by isolating verses.

**Promise Versus Principle.** For example, let's look at
the temptations of Jesus in the wilderness.

> And Jesus being full of the Holy Ghost returned from
> Jordan, and was led by the Spirit into the wilderness,
>
> Being forty days tempted of the devil. And in those
> days he did eat nothing: and when they were ended, he
> afterward hungered.
>
> And the devil said unto him, If thou be the Son of God,
> command this stone that it be made bread [Temptation #1].
>
> And Jesus answered him, saying, It is written, That
> man shall not live by bread alone, but by every word of God.
>
> And the devil, taking him up into an high mountain,
> shewed unto him all the kingdoms of the world in a moment
> of time.
>
> And the devil said unto him, All this power will I give
> thee, and the glory of them: for that is delivered unto me;
> and to whomsoever I will I give it.
>
> If thou therefore wilt worship me, all shall be thine
> [Temptation #2].
>
> And Jesus answered and said unto him, Get thee

behind me, Satan: for it is written, Thou shalt worship the
Lord thy God, and him only shalt thou serve.

And he brought him to Jerusalem, and set him on a
pinnacle of the temple, and said unto him, If thou be the
Son of God, cast thyself down from hence:

For it is written, He shall give his angels charge over
thee, to keep thee:

And in their hands they shall bear thee up, lest at any
time thou dash thy foot against a stone [Temptation #3].

And Jesus answering said unto him, It is said, Thou
shalt not tempt the Lord thy God.

And when the devil had ended all the temptation, he
departed from him for a season.

Luke 4:1-13

In each of these three temptations, Jesus quoted Scripture to deflect Satan's tempting arrows.

When Satan saw that Jesus was going to stick with
Scripture, *he got into Scripture with Him.*

- In His defense against Satan each time, Jesus quoted
  *principles* from Scripture.
- When Satan quoted Scripture, he quoted *promises.*

Notice that Jesus would not **apply a promise** taken
from Scripture if it was to be claimed in **violation of a
principle.** Do you see how treacherous Satan is with Scripture? He will take the promises of God's Word and turn it
away from principle to lead you down a trail of defeat. He
magnifies the promises; Jesus magnifies the principles. **You
cannot claim a promise if you are in violation of a principle.**

If Satan used Scripture in an effort to confuse Jesus,
certainly he will use Scripture on you. This is why we have

so many different doctrines, all taken from the same Bible. Satan has been helping people interpret Scripture. This is also the reason for so much disunity and disagreement among Christians.

If Satan can get you to claim a promise while you are in violation of a principle that relates to it, you won't receive the promise. Then Satan comes back and mocks, "See, it doesn't work," and the confusion continues.

We must learn to *rightly divide the Word of Truth* (II Timothy 2:15).

**Another Gospel.** There needs to be a clear-cut and simple way to do this, so Satan cannot confuse Christians with the Gospel. Look at what Paul the apostle said concerning this in II Corinthians 11:3.

> ...I fear, lest by any means, as the serpent beguiled Eve through his subtilty, so your minds should be corrupted from the simplicity that is in Christ.
> **II Corinthians 11:3**

Look at Galatians 1:6-7:

> I marvel that ye are so soon removed from him that called you into the grace of Christ unto another gospel:
> Which is not another; but there be some that trouble you, and would pervert the gospel of Christ.
> **Galatians 1:6-7**

What did Paul mean by "another gospel: which is not another"? Well, we learned in an earlier chapter that *Gospel* means "Good News."

That's all it means. **Good News.**

We must divide the Word of Truth to be certain that

what we are believing lines up with the Gospel (Good News) of Jesus.

**Dividing the Word Accurately.** There is no such thing as "another gospel." If *gospel* means "good news" then that is all it means. It can only be good news. You can't make it mean anything else.

Jesus sent His disciples forth with the commission, "...Go ye into all the world, and preach the gospel..." (Mark 16:15).

To put this simply...**if it is not Good News it is not Gospel.** If what you are believing is not Good News, then it is not the Gospel of Jesus. It is a "perverted gospel."

Some would say, "If you are going to preach all the Bible you will have to preach some bad news." Oh No! Not to the believer who walks in obedience.

Bad news is only for the unbelieving and disobedient. Once you are a child of God, forgiven of your sins and have stopped sinning, you should only receive Good News into your spirit man. In this world you will hear bad news, but don't receive it into your spirit, "...as others which have no hope" (I Thessalonians 4:13). I said this before, but it bears repeating here:

- Good News to a **lost man** is that he can be saved.
- Good News to a **sick man** is that he can be healed.
- Good News to a **poor man** is that he can be rich.

Can you comprehend this? God said that He would make the way so plain that "wayfaring men, though fools, shall not err therein" (Isaiah 35:8).

I am convinced that you have to be *willing* to be led away from the truth in order for Satan to confuse you and carry you away "unto vain jangling" (I Timothy 1:6).

**Ungodly Counsel.** Make up your mind to rightly divide the Word of Truth by asking yourself this question, *As an obedient believer, is this good news to me or bad news?* This will pretty well keep you on track. Remember, Psalm 1:1 warns us, "Blessed is the man that walketh not in the counsel of the ungodly...."

Ungodly counsel can come to you from someone preaching Scripture. If it disagrees with the *principle of good news/ bad news,* set it aside and don't take it into your spirit. Unless of course, you are committing willful sin. In such a case, repent and get back under the Gospel.

I close this point with a warning from Paul:

> For such are false apostles, deceitful workers, transforming themselves into the apostles of Christ.
>
> And no marvel; for Satan himself is transformed into an angel of light.
>
> Therefore it is no great thing if his ministers also be transformed as the ministers of righteousness...."
> **II Corinthians 11:13-15**

Remember, James called it "bitter and sweet water" coming out of the same source. "...Brethren, these things ought not so to be" (James 3:10-12).

Take heed to Paul's warning, "But I fear, lest by any means, as the serpent beguiled Eve through his subtlety, so your minds should be corrupted from the simplicity that is in Christ." **Revelation on the word of God always simplifies.** If an explanation on the meaning of a Scripture seems to complicate instead of simplify, you can be sure you don't have a revelation from God on it.

Remember, you are living by faith. **You don't believe the Word of God because you understand it, you begin to**

**understand it after you determine to believe it.**

Watch out for Satan when he comes as an angel of light. He seems to be most effective at doing this through someone you love or have confidence in.

Test everything you hear by this principle, "Is it **good new** or **bad news?**"

Satan will try to attack anyone. He even tried to attack God Almighty, but it didn't take God long to get rid of him. Jesus said that He "beheld Satan as lightning fall from heaven" when the Father cast him out after his attack (Luke 10:18). Now that's fast! It isn't a sin to be attacked, nor is it abnormal. We only sin when we accept defeat.

**Stolen Saxophone.** In 1983, Thelma and I were staying at a hotel in Prince Albert, Canada. The police called at 8:00 a.m. on a Sunday morning to inform us that someone had broken into our vehicle. The thief had stolen my saxophone and a long, leather topcoat.

When we found out what had been stolen, Thelma caught my hand, and looking me squarely in the eyes she said, "It's cold up here. Let them have the topcoat, but let's send out our angels to bring back the saxophone. You play that saxophone to glorify God."

We knew the Word. It was hidden in our hearts. We joined hands and resisted the devil as the thief—not a human as the thief. Then we spoke to our angels, who were given charge over us to keep us in all our ways (Psalm 91:11), and we commissioned them in the Name of Jesus to bring back my saxophone. We released the topcoat and gave it to the person who had stolen it.

Six weeks later we were back at our home in Texas, when we received a notice from the Post Office that we had a package. I applied at the window, **and do you know what it was?** The saxophone! **In perfect condition.** We never saw the topcoat again. We had released it.

You are in control when you know the Word and apply it in faith.

## Device #4: As a Bird

> Hearken; Behold, there went out a sower to sow:
>
> And it came to pass, as he sowed, some fell by the way side, and the fowls of the air came and devoured it up.
>
> **Mark 4:3-4**

**Jesus, the Teacher.** Jesus is obviously the best Teacher about recognizing Satan's devices and tactics.

In verse 15 of Mark 4, Jesus warns that when the Word (seed) is sown by the wayside, "...Satan cometh immediately, and taketh away the word that was sown in their hearts."

**The Wayside.** First let's consider the term *wayside.* Obviously, this is an unattended area. There are no scarecrows in this area to deter the devil. No special attention, effort or oversight has been given to this seed.

**You Need a Scarecrow for the Word.** Is it any wonder that we are taught specifically to study the Word and to give attendance to reading the Word?

David said, "Thy word have I hid in mine heart, that I might not sin against thee" (Psalm 119:11).

He hid it! He hid it! That takes effort. Special, concentrated effort.

You need to bury it beneath the surface. Watch over it. Water it. Fertilize it. Dig around it. Fight the devil off so he doesn't carry it away from your memory.

The best way to hide the Word in your heart is to think on it long enough to memorize passages and even chapters.

Go back over a sermon you have heard.

Buy the tapes and books on certain subjects by anointed men of God.

Repetition on a subject is the best way to bury it in your heart. Even if you were really impressed by a sermon you heard, it is said that you will only remember about ten percent of it after three days. If you hear it twice, you will remember as much as one-third of it, if you really apply yourself. But if you listen to it as much as five times, it will become a part of your nature. Then it will alter the course of your thinking patterns. It will be planted in your spirit. You will never forget that message.

When you hide the Word in your heart, you become like a scarecrow to the devil. He can no longer steal it away like a bird picks up seed sown in an unprotected zone.

**Lost Truth.** If you hear the Truth without it becoming a part of you, it is as if you never heard it. The Word must become a part of you to produce a harvest according to its potential. **"He becometh poor that dealeth with a slack hand:** but the hand of the **diligent** maketh rich" (Proverbs 10:4).

It will require concentration and special effort.

Always take notes, and be attentive to hide the Word deeply away from Satan's attempt to steal it.

**The Rewards Are Fantastic.** No sickness and untimely death (no killing). No poverty or material thieves (no stealing).

No guilt ridden conscience and separation from the constant flow of God's desire and miraculous supply (no destroying).

In the first Psalm, the entire picture is painted and displayed in "technicolor."

**Blessed is the man that walketh not in the counsel of the ungodly [or ungodly counsel, regardless of its source],**

nor standeth in the way of sinners, nor sitteth in the seat of the scornful.

But his delight is in the law of the Lord; and in his law doth he meditate day and night.

And he shall be like a tree planted by the rivers of water, *that bringeth forth his fruit in his season; his leaf also shall not wither; and whatsoever he doeth shall prosper.*

**Psalm 1:1-3**

**The Nature of a Bird.** Next, since Jesus compared Satan to a bird, let's consider the nature of a bird. Any bird. Every bird you see is constantly pursuing either one of two things. It is either pursuing food or reproduction after its kind.

Satan is interested in the same thing. If he can take away your food, then his efforts to make you like him are easily accomplished.

Our food (the Word) is our strength. "If you faint in the day of adversity, your strength is small" (Proverbs 24:10, NKJV). If you don't resist the thief he will get your food. And if he gets your food, you will have no strength to resist temptation.

Remember this: When you submit to the devil and are in his territory, you cannot stop his dirty work. **He will reproduce himself in you—stealing, killing and destroying.**

When Jesus stood on the written Word during His temptation in the wilderness, the devil departed from Him. Jesus was dried out to the devil through His knowledge of the Word in His heart. In Luke 4:13-14 Scripture records, "And...he [the devil] departed from him [Jesus] for a season. And Jesus returned in the power of the Spirit into Galilee: and there went out a fame of him through all the region round about."

Remember I John 5:18, "...But he that is begotten of God

keepeth himself [by walking in the Word day in and day out], and that wicked one toucheth him not."

NOW! Read this section again so the devil won't steal it from you.

## Device #5: Little Foxes

**Take us the foxes, the little foxes, that spoil the vines: for our vines have tender grapes.**
**Song of Solomon 2:15**

**Tender Grapes.** First the question: What are the tender grapes that the "old fox," the devil, is trying to destroy? I found the answer in Galatians 5:22-23, "But the fruit of the Spirit is love, joy, peace, longsuffering, gentleness, goodness, faith, meekness, temperance...." These grapes grow when you, "have crucified the flesh with the affections and lusts" (Galatians 5:24).

**Watch out for little foxes!**

They are so small that you might not recognize them. Zechariah 4:10 asks, "...Who hath despised the day of small things?"

**How Does the Fox Work?** Look at the procedure of the little foxes that Solomon is talking about.

Solomon (symbolic of Christ) is speaking to his espoused sweetheart (symbolic of the bride of Christ, the Church). Solomon is warning his bride about letting trivial things separate them—unimportant things that will erode their love life and bring coldness to their relationship.

Solomon uses an illustration he knows that his bride, the keeper of a grape vineyard, will understand. The baby foxes come into her fields in the heat of the day and dig around the moist roots of the vines to cool themselves.

While there, they chew on the roots to cut their young teeth. All anyone needs to do to know where the young foxes have been is to look over the fields and see the vines that are turning brown and dying.

The vine dies and ceases to produce grapes when the roots are chewed apart.

**Watch out for little foxes.**

Solomon warns in Proverbs 28:13, "He that covereth his sins shall not prosper...."

If you know of things in your life that are working against your spiritual progress, believe me, they are not that important. When God saved you, He only took away the things that were working against you.

If your conscience convicts you of something, stop doing it. Stop allowing that action to happen. **Just stop!** No one else may know about it but you and God; however, it is hurting your grape production (the fruits of the Spirit).

I like the words of a song I heard many years ago.

## The Trade

I traded my sins for salvation,
I traded my load for relief,
I obtained peace for my condemnation,
And the joy of the Lord for my grief.
I traded a life that was wasted,
For a temple to dwell in God made.
What I got was so much more,
than what he received.
I am sure I got the best of the trade.

Author Unknown

Turn loose of the old lifestyle. It doesn't fit with your

new life. God has so much better for you. Things you classify as little can ruin your prosperity in God and can open the door to Satan to **steal, kill and destroy** in your life.

**Lot's Loss.** A good illustration is Abraham's nephew, Lot. When God delivered Lot and his family out of Sodom and Gomorrah just prior to its annihilation, He told them to go immediately into the mountains. Lot began his journey toward the mountains, but sought a lower zone to dwell in. Thus he began looking around Bela, a town he was traveling through on his journey. The name *Bela* means "little," which he quickly pointed out to God when asking permission to stop short of the mountains (Genesis 19:18-22; 14:2).

Lot stopped short of what God had told him to do. This left him in view of Sodom and Gomorrah. But he had been warned by God not to look back lest he die. Had Lot followed God's instructions all the way, he would have been out of view of the city. His wife, then, could not have looked back and died. You see, when the fire began to fall from Heaven to destroy the wicked cities, Lot's wife turned to look at it and immediately became a pillar of salt.

Lot lost his wife to death, all because he stopped his journey to the mountain of God's calling in preference for something he called "little."

When you minimize sin you also will fail to make an effort to stop it.

Now go back and read again the verses in Galatians on the fruit of the Spirit. If you are lacking in the production of any of these grapes, it could very well be "little foxes." You could be allowing something to continue in your life that is preventing you from moving on up with God. This can be what is stopping your flow of blessings.

Let the Holy Ghost speak to you here and now.

Satan will always minimize sin and magnify the toughness of dwelling in the mountain.

It isn't hard to produce the fruit of the Spirit when you abandon sin and live close to God. The fruit just naturally grows.

**Watch out for little foxes.**

Remember, "He that covereth his sin shall not prosper..." (Proverbs 28:13).

## Jesus Never Lost

Jesus knew everything there was to know about Satan. Therefore, He never took a loss at Satan's hands. (His death and substitutionary sufferings, of course, were deliberate and on your behalf.)

Satan obeyed Jesus' every command. When He said, **"Go!"** The devils even asked permission about which way to go, such as when the legion of devils went into the herd of swine (Matthew 8:31).

## Summary

You have to know Satan's devices and walk in authority over him before you can stop his **stealing, killing and destroying.**

These five devices listed above are not the only descriptions of Satan found in Scripture. He is also referred to as a serpent, a scorpion and a dragon. Study their natures, and you will know more about Satan's methods and tactics.

Again, remember I John 5:18, "...But he that is begotten of God keepeth himself, and that wicked one toucheth him not."

Then you can say, "Surely goodness and mercy shall

follow me all the days of my life: and I will dwell in the house of the Lord for ever" (Psalm 23:6).

**We are not exempt from being attacked, but we are redeemed from being losers.**

# 10

# Due Season, Tough Times and Light Afflictions

The Apostle Paul encourages us in Galatians 6:9, "And let us not be weary in well doing: for in *due season* we shall reap, if we *faint* not." Knowing the comfort God intended in these words for His children, let's consider some important questions about this passage.

## Due Season?

What is *due season?*
How can I know when that is?
How long does it take to get there?
What is meant by *fainting?*
If God really wants me to walk in goodness and mercy all the days of my life, according to Psalm 23:6, why do things get so tough?
I can handle the little problems. But what about those in which imminent death or bankruptcy threatens? What about other problems that continue like a marathon? How long will this go on? I will address all these questions in this chapter.

# The Good Fight of Faith

Paul admonishes us to "fight the good fight of faith..." (I Timothy 6:12). Thank God it is a good fight. When we fight in faith, we know we will win. That's what makes it a **good** fight. But, alas, it **is a battle.** And you must realize that some battles last longer than others. However, **if we don't quit, God won't quit.** God spoke this to my spirit during a severe spiritual battle. **All you have to do to defeat the devil is to be more determined than he is.** The author of Proverbs 23:18 observes, "...Surely there is an end...."

Let's talk about *due season.* This is a time we are all interested in. When is my payday going to arrive?

# The Fullness of Time

Scripture says of God, "...The husbandman waiteth for the precious fruit of the earth, and hath long patience for it..." (James 5:7). "But when the fulness of the time was come, God sent forth his Son..." (Galatians 4:4). That took place about 4,000 years after God made His initial statement and plans.

God began to reap His harvest in only three days after He had sown His seed, Jesus. When Jesus rose from the dead, graves all over Jerusalem burst open, and God began to receive His harvest. However, today the harvest is still not complete—nearly 2,000 years later. But the Word of God tells us that He has "patience for it."

Our harvest time depends on a lot of things, but it initially depends on **what type of seed we sow.** If you sow mushrooms, your harvest will come up overnight. However if you want an oak tree, you must sow an acorn, and that is going to take more time. A mushroom, when grown, can be kicked over by your foot. You can't do that to an oak tree. Think about the kind of seed you are sowing. This will help you determine your due season.

What are you sowing toward?

The following story will help you keep your faith and have patience.

## My Son, Jerry, an Oak Tree

In 1968, while pastoring a church in Houston, Texas, I heard about a conference on *Soul Winning* being conducted by two Baptist preachers, John R. Rice and Dr. Jack Hyles. Jack Hyles was known as the leading teacher in one-on-one soul winning of that time. I went and gathered all their materials together after listening intently to them for two days. They taught and preached with tears dripping from their chins. I was stirred to the core of my being. It seemed I could feel the throbbing of God's heart.

When I returned home, I gathered all the materials I could find on the subject. I ordered all of T.L. Osborn's materials, including banners and posters. I hung them all over the church—"Soul Winning—Out Where The Sinners Are." I began teaching soul winning, as well as preaching and practicing it before the people.

Practice sessions were organized on Tuesday nights, so the church members could develop their confidence and overcome their fears. We memorized a set of seven lead-in questions which had been wisely and carefully arranged. Regardless of the answers given, soul winners could go to the next question. In this manner, church members could bring a person to a decision for Christ before the conversation was ended.

I taught soul winning! I preached it! I stayed with this

subject for six months...in almost every service. I was determined to make our congregation into a soul winning force. But people began to drop out of church. They didn't want to complain because they knew this message was right, yet they wouldn't get with it. Regardless of my intensity, I could not seem to get soul winning off the ground.

Instead of the church growing, we started losing people. I felt that I was a failure in this area, so I shifted back to a more customary and standard type of ministry. However, I bore this feeling of failure until 1987.

Here is what happened 19 years later.

My son, Jerry Davis, President of Street Reach Ministries, Inc., held a soul winning blitz on the beaches of Padre Island, Texas. Afterward, he and I sat in my den and discussed his work. A minister friend and his wife, who were our house guests at the time, joined in our conversation and watched as my son showed us a video of his ministry activities on the beach. I watched as he talked to a man about Jesus. Jerry had his arm around the fellow who was in a bathing suit with a beer can in one hand and a cigarette in the other. To my surprise, Jerry was using that set of seven questions I had taught 20 years prior. I leaned forward in my chair and my mouth fell open.

I knew Jerry was a soul winner and had been for more than 15 years. But when I heard him using that set of seven questions, something inside me jumped. I turned to my pastor friend and exclaimed, "Twenty years ago I used to teach that to my church, but I never could get anybody to go with it. I finally dropped it with a feeling of failure." Jerry whirled around with the strangest look on his face.

"Dad!" he exclaimed. "That's where I got all of this."

Jerry was eleven years old when I taught soul winning to our church. I never knew until 20 years later the effect that my teaching had on his life. Now, soul winning is my oldest son's full-time ministry. Today, he has one of the best known and most effective soul winning ministries of our time. He is often seen on Trinity Broadcasting Network with attorney Jay Sekulow. Needless to say, I have given up feeling like a failure.

I didn't realize it at that time, but I had apparently based my thinking on immediate results. I hadn't allowed for the growing of an oak tree. I wanted mushroom growth. I must admit, I am totally fulfilled with my oak tree. Jerry personally is winning thousands of people to the Lord, plus passing on the teaching to others with manuals he has developed on the subject.[1]

# Detecting a Faint

Things of great value develop for you when you sow seeds and then exercise your faith and patience. However, Galatians warns that *fainting* will hinder your harvest. To *faint* means simply to grow impatient. This is when the temptation to quit gets very strong. You can detect fainting by listening for statements coming out of your mouth such as:

- "I don't know how much longer I can take this."
- "I'm just tired of trying anymore."
- "It doesn't matter what I do, nothing works."

Listen to yourself talk. Your words will tell you how close you are to fainting.

Fainting opens the door to fear and, therefore, failure.

---

[1] *For more information about my son's ministry and his anointed materials, please refer to the back pages of this book.*

Remember the words of Solomon in Proverbs, "In all labour there is profit: but the talk of the lips tendeth only to penury" (Proverbs 14:23).

**Fainting never wins, and winners never faint.**

The reason that a farmer sows seed is so he can reap a harvest. A farmer has to have faith. He must believe that when he gives his seed to the ground, the ground will develop it for him. Then in **due season** the ground will give it back to him in far more abundance than he originally gave. The farmer plans in advance for the period between sowing and reaping. He may have to be extremely frugal in that period and exercise great restraint on his spending. But even before he sows his seed he plows his ground in hope.

**He prepares for his harvest before he even plants.**

You need to have that kind of faith in God. He is Good Soil. Plow with God before you sow your seed. Make sure your relationship with Him is correct and pollution free. It takes good soil to grow good crops. *The condition of the ground makes a great deal of difference in how fast a crop grows.*

## Sowing in Good Ground

Look at it this way.

Scripture teaches, "Whatsoever ye do, do it heartily, as to the Lord, and not unto men" (Colossians 3:23). Herein lies one of the biggest problems with sowing for some people. **Too many people do their giving as UNTO MAN and not as unto the Lord.** The root of bitterness develops, when they don't see an immediate, abundant harvest. Consequently, many people become disappointed in the individual or ministry that they gave to. When this happens, you can be sure that their soil was man, not God!

Even if an individual or ministry is above reproach, it is not wise to give as unto man. Man's soil is not as good as

166

God's. **Always give as unto the Lord.** Then if the earthly recipient disappoints you, it won't become a problem to you. **The soil you sowed in was God.** This way your harvest is not affected. When you plow with God, you are actually plowing up your own "fallow ground" (Jeremiah 4:3).

In Isaiah 40:3 we are admonished:

> ...Prepare ye the way of the Lord, make straight in the desert a highway for our God.
>
> Isaiah 40:3

God doesn't need cultivating, but we do. The actual truth is, we are sowing in our own soil when we give as unto the Lord. You can do something about your soil. However, you can't control the soil of someone else's life.

Too many of us can sadly quote, "...They made me the keeper of the vineyards; but mine own vineyard have I not kept" (Song of Solomon 1:6). If I judge myself, I can do something about it. But if I judge others, I can do nothing more.

**Spend your energy plowing your own ground.** Make it ready for God to bless. Remember, "...The prosperity of fools shall destroy them" (Proverbs 1:32). When you give as unto the Lord, you are planting in your own soil. I know this is true because you are the one who reaps the harvest. When a hired hand sows in another man's field, the harvest still belongs to the owner of that field.

**Sow as unto the Lord, and the harvest will come back to you.**

## Hastening Due Season

You can actually cause **due season** to accelerate and

even get a bumper crop, if *your soil is in excellent condition.* It needs a good balance of proper ingredients. Natural ground needs iron and zinc to produce most effectively from the seed sown in it.

The soil of your heart needs lots of *love.* It also needs *hope* and *faith.* You need to cultivate these ingredients if there is a lack of them. A good farmer uses additives when he discovers an imbalance in the soil.

If he also discovers adverse ingredients he deals with these, too. Likewise, you must remove any adverse ingredients in your life: *Hate, bitterness, unforgiveness, strife, envy, greed, malice, selfish pride, arrogance, haughtiness and **impatience** which is childishness.*

As you grow up in the Lord and begin to mature, you put away childish things. You can then:

1. Set goals
2. Purpose in your heart (make decisions) about what you want to sow toward
3. Cultivate your soil, and prepare yourself for God to do His part
4. Make sure you don't fall into the category of a fool

You must abandon foolishness so that prosperity will not destroy you. God is not concerned with financial loss. He can cover all your mistakes and not be affected, but He doesn't want to lose *you.* Putting too much money into the hands of a fool could destroy many people, including the possessor of it.

Remember Jesus' parable of the rich fool who built bigger barns. His problem was simple to see.

> And one of the company said unto him, Master, speak to my brother, that he divide the inheritance with me.
>
> And he [Jesus] said unto him, Man, who made me a judge or a divider over you?
>
> ...Take heed, and beware of covetousness: for a man's life consisteth not in the abundance of the things which he possesseth.
>
> And he spake a parable unto them, saying, The ground of a certain rich man brought forth plentifully:
>
> And he thought within himself, saying, What shall I do, because I have no room where to bestow my fruits?
>
> And he said, This will I do: I will pull down my barns, and build greater; and there will I bestow all my fruits and my goods.
>
> And I will say to my soul, Soul, thou hast much goods laid up for many years; take thine ease, eat, drink, and be merry.
>
> But God said unto him, Thou fool, this night thy soul shall be required of thee: then whose shall those things be, which thou hast provided?
>
> So is he that layeth up treasure for himself, and is not rich toward God.
>
> **Luke 12:13-21**

This is the same problem that ruins many rich people today and renders them ineffective for God. **The man thought money was security.**

What a fool!

Security is **having faith in the integrity of God alone.** If you have a problem with that in your spirit, you will know you still have some plowing to do. **In due season we will reap if we don't faint.**

God loves you too much to give you something that would destroy you. Prove yourself trustworthy with what you do have, and God will then trust you with more.

# Tough Times

Now, **what about tough times?**
Observe what Paul said in II Corinthians 4:8-9.

> **We are troubled on every side, yet not distressed; we are perplexed, but not in despair;**
> **Persecuted, but not forsaken; cast down, but not destroyed.**
>
> **II Corinthians 4:8-9**

In short, you are constantly facing opposition and discouraging dilemmas, but you must refuse to be affected or moved from your resolve.

Tough times build spiritual muscle. They either make you bitter or better. What happens to you during tough times depends on what you consist of.

The same sun that hardens clay melts butter.

David said, "My soul is continually in my hand..." (Psalm 119:109). You alone make the decision as to whether tough times will make you bitter or better. Ask God to help your attitude.

Draw strength from Joseph's statement to his brothers, 17 years after they sold him as a slave. Tearfully they apologized for what they had done, but he cheered them with this thought: "You meant it for evil, but God meant it for good" (Genesis 50:20, paraphrased). God was building and developing Joseph's muscle and tempering his mettle. All this was so that he could handle the prosperity God had promised him 17 years before.

# An Explosive Pastoring Experience

At the age of 27, I was elected pastor of a congregation. At the time of my election in 1964, I was busy with a traveling ministry that was taking me to the top in my denomination. Suddenly, I found myself suffering severely under a barrage of heavy guns.

The former pastor of that church had retired, and the head deacon had taken the microphone from him and told him to sit down. The former pastor was a very successful and respected man in our denomination. In less than six months after I was elected, a faction in the congregation set about to get rid of me.

Unabashedly I preached against sin in every service. God would not release me from preaching this message. Little did I know what kind of sin and wrongdoing was going on among this faction. But God did. They quickly grew tired of the constant effort of the Holy Ghost to clean them up. So, because they were not willing to correct their hypocrisy, this faction prepared a petition to move me out. I didn't understand it. I couldn't sleep. *Why did they want to get rid of me?*

One day, I went to the church in the middle of the afternoon, and lay down on the floor. I tried to pray, but my body physically hurt. My legs cramped. I pulled them up in my arms, squeezed them and stretched them out, over and over. It was hard to pray or even think, so I just mostly groaned.

Finally I said, "Father, I don't understand it. I was doing so good until You sent me here. I know I came here in Your will. Why is this happening to me? I can't bear it. You promised that You would not put more on us than we are able to bear. This is *too* much! This is just **too much!!"**

I lay there in still silence. God began to talk to me. I know this experience will be a help to many others. The first thing I heard in my spirit was the question: "Who made you?" It was so clear that it almost startled me. I knew it was God.

I responded, "You did, God."

Then another question, "How many hairs do you have on your head?"

"I don't know," I answered.

Another question followed, "When are you going to die?"

Again I replied, "I don't know."

The next question, "What is going to happen in your life tomorrow?"

"I don't know."

Then came His next statement, "If I made you, I know how many hairs you have on your head. I know when you are going to die, and I know what is going to happen in your life tomorrow. Don't you think I should be the judge of how much you can bear?"

Now He had my attention! God, my loving Father, continued, "You see, I needed someone I could trust. Someone who would not turn and run. Someone to come here and clean out this corruption. I picked and sent you. Don't you see, I chose you because I knew I could trust you. The truth is, I have more confidence in you than you have in yourself. Hold your ground and I will bring you out on top of this."

I stood up in total silence. Those words from God had transformed my attitude. God had confidence in me! God could trust me! Now I understood what He was doing! Instantly the stress was gone. My legs stopped hurting. I suddenly felt like I was ten feet tall. I felt like I could go bear hunting with a switch. God trusted me!!

I walked out of that church building with a different point of view. The battle was not over, but I had my spirit under control. No more fear or complaining. As sure as God had promised, the opposition lost momentum. The faction was exposed and left the church. I continued there for several years in peace with a good, effective ministry.

## Troubles Work for Us

God knows your strengths and your weaknesses. Whatever you are facing is not more than you can handle. Ask God for His strength. Remember, He knows what you don't know. Mary and Martha thought Jesus had come too late to meet their need (John 11:1-44). Perhaps you would have agreed. But Jesus knew what they didn't know. He also knows what you don't know.

If you want to see what no one has seen, you must face what no one has faced. You will **never** get a miracle until you need one. I draw from Paul's understanding in II Corinthians 4:16-17.

> ...We faint not; but though our outward man perish, yet the inward man is renewed day by day.
>
> For our light affliction, which is but for a moment, *worketh for us* a far more exceeding and eternal weight of glory.
>
> **II Corinthians 4:16-17**

Notice those words, **"worketh for us."**

Do you believe that? Can you make your troubles become your servant? Can you understand that they are working together for your good? If you really believe this, then you will rejoice from your heart. And that, of course, is

173

the scriptural thing to do.

- Stay out of fear
- Maintain your faith

You can't lose for winning if you live and function in winning principles.

Speak it loud enough for your ears to hear, **tough times are working for me—not against me!!**

Remember: If you want to **see** miracles, you must first be willing to **need** them.

## Light Afflictions

Now, let's talk about **light afflictions.** Light afflictions I can handle. But what about those life-threatening, bankruptcy-threatening situations. How long, O Lord, how long? What about those heavy afflictions?

Question: How do we determine the difference between light and heavy?

What is extremely heavy for a 90-pound weakling would be very lightweight to a 245-pound weight lifter. You alone must determine what is heavy or light by your own spiritual muscle.

Let's observe what Paul called light afflictions. In II Corinthians 11:23-28, he lists examples of the light afflictions that he personally faced in the process of serving God:

- Abundant labors
- Stripes above measure [Paul was beaten so much that he lost count.]
- In prisons frequently
- At the point of death often

- Beaten by the Jews five times with 39 stripes [Those were only the beatings from the Jews.]
- Three times beaten with rods
- Stoned and left for dead
- Shipwrecked three times [Paul called these "light afflictions."]
- A night and a day in the ocean [with sharks]
- "In journeyings often, in perils of waters, in perils of robbers, in perils by mine own countrymen"
- In perils by the heathen
- In perils among false brethren [hypocrites]
- In weariness and painfulness, in hunger and thirst, in cold and nakedness
- Plus, the care of all the churches [One seems to be plenty for most preachers.]

Yet in verse 29, Paul concluded, "...I am...offended, and I burn not."

He said in Acts 20:22-24, "...I go bound in the spirit unto Jerusalem, not knowing the things that shall befall me there: Save that the Holy Ghost witnesseth in every city, saying that bonds and afflictions abide me. But none of these things move me...."

We must come to that point of determination, or we will never become stabilized in the Word. Only if God can trust us, will He give us responsibility. But remember, **responsibility also comes with privilege.**

Remember what Shadrach, Meshach, and Abednego said to King Nebuchadnezzar, "Our God whom we serve is able to deliver us, but if not, we will not bow to your golden calf" (Daniel 3:17-18, paraphrased). Because of this trustworthy attitude, not only were they delivered from the fire, but they were promoted to the leadership of the nation.

We need to declare our afflictions to be light because, "...the sufferings of this present time are not worthy to be compared with the glory which shall be revealed in us" (Romans 8:18).

In Deuteronomy 8, God gave His chosen people some staggering but glorious and abundant promises.

> For the Lord thy God bringeth thee into a good land, a land of brooks of water, of fountains and depths that spring out of valleys and hills;
>
> A land of wheat, and barley, and vines, and fig trees, and pomegranates; a land of oil olive, and honey;
>
> A land wherein thou shalt eat bread without scarceness, thou shalt not lack any thing in it; a land whose stones are iron, and out of whose hills thou mayest dig brass.
>
> ...when thou hast eaten and art full, and hast built goodly houses, and dwelt therein;
>
> And when thy herds and thy flocks multiply, and thy silver and thy gold is multiplied, and all that thou hast is multiplied.
>
> But thou shalt remember the Lord thy God: for it is he that giveth thee power to get wealth, that he may establish his covenant which he sware unto thy fathers, as it is this day.
>
> Deuteronomy 8:7-9, 12-13, 18

After observing all these abundant promises, go back to verses 2 and 3.

> And thou shalt remember *all the way* which the Lord thy God led thee these forty years in the wilderness, *to humble thee,* and *to prove thee,* to *know what was in thine heart,* whether thou wouldest keep his commandments, or no.
>
> And , *he humbled thee,* and *he suffered thee to hunger,*

**and fed thee with manna, which thou knewest not, neither did thy fathers know; that he might make thee know that man doth not live by bread only, but by every word that proceedeth out of the mouth of the Lord doth man live.**
**Deuteronomy 8:2-3**

Remember the snakes, the bitter water, lack of water and all the problems the Children of Israel suffered, including no stores to purchase food from. God was their only Source.

# God's Discipline and Provision

God led the Children of Israel through all these hardships—and blessed them in the midst of trouble—to teach them to lean on Him as their Source. Let's reflect on several specific ways that God led the Children of Israel...and some of **the ways that He leads *you!***

At the last minute, so to speak, God parted the Red Sea and saved the Children of Israel from the pursuing Egyptians (Exodus 14). This was a miracle they had never seen before. **Here, God demonstrated that when there seems to be no way out, He will provide the way of escape...and *always* at the perfect time!**

God led the Children of Israel to much needed water only to discover that it was bitter or poison (Exodus 15:22-27). Then by a miracle He sweetened the water. **God used this lesson to show His Children that no security exists outside of dependency on Him.**

God led the Children of Israel through a wilderness where nothing grew, where they had to depend on Him for every bite of food (Exodus 16:1-21). They could not even save leftovers for the next day. The Children of Israel had to depend on God for their DAILY bread. God deliberately put them in this position so that He could prove His faithfulness to them daily. **He wanted His children to learn that they could trust Him to provide their *every* need every day.**

When God let the Children of Israel run out of water in the desert, they did not know where to go (Exodus 17:1-7). The Red Sea was behind them, and the desert lay ahead of them. Moreover, He gave them water from a most unlikely place: a rock. And this He did supernaturally and *abundantly*. **Here, God demonstrated that when His Children's supply is exhausted, He will create a new and abundant supply—even if it is from a surprising and unlikely source.**

The Children of Israel won wars that were impossible such as at Jericho (Joshua 6:1-21), and lost wars that appeared to be easy such as at Ai (Joshua 7). The lesson was: **They could do anything when they followed His instruction, but could not do the simplest thing when they disobeyed God.**

God's obvious purpose in leading the Children of Israel in all these ways was to prove (test) them. He wanted to see if they would live and make decisions "...by every word that proceedeth out of the mouth of the Lord..." (Deuteronomy 8:3). In verse 5 He tells them, "...As a man chasteneth his son, so the Lord thy God chasteneth thee." Then in verse 16, God sums up His reasons for leading them through all this: "...That he might humble thee, and that he might prove thee, to *do thee good at thy latter end.*" **God is planning *good* things for you. But He will qualify you first.**

Remember, "...the prosperity of fools shall destroy them" (Proverbs 1:32). You can only eliminate foolishness when you **abandon your ways and your thoughts in favor of doing things God's way.** But you must do this with absolute faith in God's integrity.

Was God cruel to treat the Children of Israel the way He did? Obviously not; He did it for their good. Their ways would have brought them total defeat and annihilation. But **God loved them too much to leave them to their own ways.**

## Search Your Spirit

Don't be impatient. In the middle of those extremely difficult battles of faith that you go through, look for answers to the questions in your mind. But do it in faith.

Begin to praise and glorify God. Tell Him that you trust Him. Cease to complain. Start expecting things to change. Remind Him of His promises and then thank Him for their fulfillment in advance. Remember, "...weeping may endure for a night, but joy cometh in the morning" (Psalm 30:5).

**Love, faith, hope and praise** are four anchors that will hold your ship in the midst of any storm. You will reap **in due season** if you don't pull anchor or faint. When Paul's ship was near destruction on a storming ocean, "...they cast *four* anchors out of the stern, and wished for the day" (Acts 27:29). Remember, your four anchors are *love, faith, hope and praise.*

I like the words of Job when facing a devastating situation, "...He knoweth the way that I take: when he hath tried me, I shall come forth as gold" (Job 23:10). Job became twice as rich as he was before Satan's attack.

**...Keep up the faith talk....**

## Personal Experience

I made a statement of faith to God when I began my traveling ministry. "Father, if You can get the money to me at all, You can get it to me on the due date." To me *due season* was the *due date,* the date that I needed the money.

On one occasion, I had paid all my bills except one $1,000 note, which was due on the first of each month. This particular day was a Monday morning, the first day of the month—a full week before any more money was scheduled to arrive. On that morning, I rose early to pray about the shortage. While sitting at my desk, I reminded God of my faith position: I believed that His Word concerning *due season* meant that He would provide what I needed on my *due date*...**that very day!**

While I sat there reminding Him, the phone rang. It was 7:15 a.m., and a prayer ministry partner was calling. He needed prayer about a domestic problem that he was having. We prayed. When I finished I asked him if he would agree with me about my situation. I then explained it without giving him the amount. He responded, "Why sure, how much is it that you need?"

I told him that I didn't want to divulge the amount. I had already told God, and I just needed his prayer of agreement. So he prayed a strong prayer. Then he asked again, "How much do you need?"

Again I refused to tell him, so he asked, "Would $2,000 help?

I replied, "It would help a bunch."

He assured me that he would call me back in 30 minutes and tell me if the deal he was working on was ready. If so, he would give me the money. He called back and asked me to meet him at noon. I had the money in my hands by 12:30 p.m., and my bill was paid on the due date with $1000 left over! This covered another unexpected bill of $600 that had suddenly developed that day. If I had told the man how much I needed I would have gotten $1,000 dollars, but would have been $600 short. As it was I had enough to also cover the $600 with $400 left over.

God meets us at the point of our faith. He will "...do exceeding abundantly above all that we ask or think..." (Ephesians 3:20). If you lean on man you will be limited. If you look to God He will give you more than enough.

## Summary

As you await your **due season**—*the choice is yours!!*

**Choose** to prepare, sow and believe for your results with **God** in mind, **not man.** Decide that you are only going to sow *godly* seeds. Make sure that your needs, desires and goals are centered in God's will. Believe that the plans you have made for the time between sowing and reaping are providing a foundation for the "long haul." Then fight the *good* fight of faith, going forth *assured* by the Word of God.

**Choose** to hasten your **due season** by tending the soil of your heart, by cultivating the fruits of the Spirit...love, joy, peace, patience, etc. Be *adamant* in your decision to refuse to permit the enemy to claim any part of your sowing field.

**Choose** to develop a *steadfast* attitude about the integrity of God and His faithfulness to see you through. When you do, you will *know* that any tough times you encounter are working *for* you, not *against* you. Be sure to praise and thank God for the fulfillment of your miracle **as you wait.**

Then, in the fullness of time, **you will prevail!**

# 11

# What to Do if Your Brook Dries Up!

"Everything *was* going along pretty smoothly in my life, but suddenly it seems like things are beginning to fall apart. I can't seem to do anything right. It's like the bottom is dropping out. I don't know of anything I am doing differently. I can't figure it out. It seems like God has abandoned me." Does that sound familiar?

> Beloved, think it not strange concerning the fiery trial which *is to try you*, as though some strange thing happened unto you: But rejoice....
>
> **I Peter 4:12-13**

This chapter is written for two categories of people: Those who have had their brooks dry up, and for those who **will** face a similar situation. **Don't think it strange,** Peter taught.

In Colossians Paul said, "...Your life is hid with Christ in God" (Colossians 3:3). If that is true how can Satan get to you?

# It May Not Be Caused by the Devil

I want you to see something with me. Satan may not be involved at all. Let's consider two people who had their brooks dry up at the same time. Observe with me what was done to open up the fountain of provision again. The incident is recorded in I Kings 17:1-16.

> And Elijah the Tishbite, who was of the inhabitants of Gilead, said unto Ahab, As the Lord God of Israel liveth, before whom I stand, there shall not be dew nor rain these years, but according to my word.
>
> And the word of the Lord came unto him, saying,
>
> Get thee hence, and turn thee eastward, and hide thyself by the brook Cherith, that is before Jordan.
>
> And it shall be, that thou shalt drink of the brook; and I have commanded the ravens to feed thee there.
>
> So he went and did according unto the word of the Lord: for he went and dwelt by the brook Cherith, that is before Jordan.
>
> And the ravens brought him bread and flesh in the morning, and bread and flesh in the evening; and he drank of the brook.
>
> And it came to pass after a while, that the brook dried up, because there had been no rain in the land.
>
> And the word of the Lord came unto him, saying,
>
> Arise, get thee to Zarephath, which belongeth to Zidon, and dwell there: behold, I have commanded a widow woman there to sustain thee.
>
> So he arose and went to Zarephath. And when he came to the gate of the city, behold, the widow woman was there gathering of sticks: and he called to her, and said, Fetch me, I pray thee, a little water in a vessel, that I may drink.
>
> And as she was going to fetch it, he called to her, and said, Bring me, I pray thee, a morsel of bread in thine hand.

And she said, As the Lord thy God liveth, I have not a cake, but an handful of meal in a barrel, and a little oil in a cruse: and, behold, I am gathering two sticks, that I may go in and dress it for me and my son, that we may eat it, and die.

And Elijah said unto her, Fear not; go and do as thou hast said: but make me thereof a little cake first, and bring it unto me, and after make for thee and for thy son.

For thus saith the Lord God of Israel, The barrel of meal shall not waste, neither shall the cruse of oil fail, until the day that the Lord sendeth rain upon the earth.

And she went and did according to the saying of Elijah: and she and he, and her house, did eat many days.

And the barrel of meal wasted not, neither did the cruse of oil fail, according to the word of the Lord, which he spake by Elijah.

I Kings 17:1-16

# Elijah—Man of Faith and Power

Let me paraphrase this story to help make it easier to understand my point.

No one was bolder than Elijah. He walked right into the king's court uninvited and made a faith announcement! "It is not going to rain until I tell it to. And I won't tell it to until this nation, beginning with the King, stops serving these gods of Baal and turns back to the Living God."

There he stood in his leather girdle, honey still in his beard. Confidence personified. The king slowly leaned forward on his throne and asked, "Who are you?"

"My name is Elijah."

"Where are you from?" continued the king.

"Tish," announced the prophet.

This is about the only time Tish is mentioned in the Bible. He was "a nobody from nowhere." The king's entire court must have echoed with the laughter. The general thought was, *Who does "Whiskers" think he is, coming in here announcing that he has control over the rain?*

Elijah turned to walk out. When he reached the door he turned and repeated: "Elijah. You had better remember the name because you are going to want me."

I love to study this man. He had such authority, boldness **and faith.**

He carried a torch for revival. He knew God. He knew that people were headed for loss, sorrow and suffering if they didn't turn. So he got drastic in faith. "When it doesn't rain, I'll get their attention. When I have their attention they will listen to what I have to say." He had the message of restoration and revival in him already, but nobody wanted to hear it.

God knows how to prepare us to hear what he wants to say. When Elijah walked into the street he prayed: "Father, now that I have made my announcement to the king, where do I go? What do I do? If it doesn't rain, crops don't grow. If food doesn't grow, people don't eat. When people can't eat, they get angry. They are going to be looking for me. It will be a long drought before they are ready to repent. What will I eat? What will I drink? I can't afford to mix with them until they are ready to repent."

## God Prepares Ahead

I love God's directive here. "Get thee hence, and turn thee eastward, and hide thyself by the brook Cherith, that is before Jordan. And it shall be, that thou shalt drink of the brook; and I have commanded the ravens to feed thee there" (I Kings 17:3-4). Those words "have commanded" bless me. Before you ever make your step of faith God has already made arrangements to provide for you.

Six months later, I can see Elijah as he peers through the

bushes, watching the search parties combing the countryside, looking for him. I get amused when I think about it. Six months ago he was a nobody from nowhere. Now, he is the most sought-after preacher in the nation. And he only preached about a five-minute message. **Little** is **much** when God is in it.

# When Everything Is Going Well

There Elijah sat, nestled in that comfortable little place, hidden by God. Birds were coming twice a day with food. Fresh water flowed from a little spring that kept his brook running regardless of the drought.

Don't you love it when things are going well?

Today, in our society, people complain about lack. Yet, even when the economy goes sour, you are provided for. Your faith is working. You have done your part, now God is obviously doing His part! Others have lost jobs, but you are still working. Others talk of cuts, but you got a raise.

You come home from work and relax in your easy chair. Your spouse brings you something cold to drink. You touch the remote control and the TV works just like it's supposed to. You planned your work, and worked your plan. It worked out just like you planned it. I love it when things are going well.

But now consider Elijah. There he sat, stretched out in the sun. People everywhere were doing without, but not him. The brook still flowed and his faithful bird servants dropped food in his lap twice a day, right on time. I can hear his mind ticking, "Sure pays to serve God. One of these days those people out there are going to get enough of their poverty, then they will be ready to listen to me."

Watch him now, as he rolls lazily over toward the brook, just as the sun is peeking over the mountaintop. He reaches over still half asleep, and drops his hand down into the brook to wash his face and clear his eyes. But, instead of water, he comes up with a handful of mud.

## A Sudden Change

Quickly he sits up. His eyes are wide open now. He stares into the brook. **No water!** "Dear God!" he exclaims, "Where is my water?" Then the full realization begins to hit him. "Here I am in the middle of the desert, and no water. I'm a wanted man. I can't go into town, they'd kill me. Besides, they don't have water either." He ponders his situation. "This can't be true. I came here in the will of God. Why has my brook dried up?"

Suddenly he notices that the birds weren't coming anymore. Have you ever noticed that when things start to fall apart, they come loose at every seam? Elijah was in the perfect will of God, yet his brook dried up. He had followed all of God's instructions, but his brook dried up. Did the devil do it? Obviously not. In fact, his brook dried up **as a result of his own faith ministry.** It was he who stopped the rain. When rain stops, brooks dry up. Who stopped the birds from coming? The same God who let the brook dry up. Why did his brook dry up and the birds stop coming?

## Why? Why?

I do not believe that God will close one door in the life of His children without opening another. Yes, things go wrong because of the things we do wrong. Solomon said, "Evil pursueth sinners..." (Proverbs 13:21). But just because the brook dries up for one of God's children doesn't necessarily mean that there was sin involved. Elijah would never have moved from that location as long as everything was going smoothly. It took a dried up brook and a lack of food to get his attention so God could give him something better.

Elijah's brook dried up so God could take him where he would have some human company. (After two-and-one-half years in a desert by yourself, one could get lonesome.) It would still be another year before the people would be ready to repent. Elijah had been idle long enough. God wanted to make him a blessing to someone else. People needed to be ministered to. Somebody was praying for help. They needed Elijah's ministry.

If you have had your brook dry up, don't despair, God has something better for you. In the words of the song writer, G.A. Young, "...God leads His dear children along. Some thro' the waters, some thro' the flood, some thro' the fire, but all thro' the Blood; Some thro' great sorrow, but God gives a song. In the night season and all the day long."[1]

God leads us all in a variety of ways through faith in Jesus Christ and His provision for our redemption.

Elijah was a man just as we are, so it states in James 5:17. But he cried out to God amid all his confusion and unrest.

However, he first must have questioned why. Do you suppose that he also tried digging in the brook? He must have thought, "Surely there is water somewhere. God wouldn't just abandon me here. Oh, God, help me!"

Consider with me what to do if *your* brook dries up.

## Number One: Don't Panic

Don't panic. The Bible warns, "Do not be afraid of sudden fear [panic]..." (Proverbs 3:25). Panic will cause you

[1] Young, G.A. *God Leads Us Along.* Lillenas Publishing Company, Kansas City.

to hurt yourself. This reminds me of a lady who once said about a harmless snake, "Well, he may not hurt me, but he sure could make me hurt myself."

We've all heard the comment, "I've got to do something even if I do it wrong." That's panic. The best posture to take when you don't know what to do is to do nothing until you hear from God. Pray and seek His face. In Jeremiah 33:3 God said, "Call unto me, and I will answer thee, and shew thee great and mighty things, which thou knowest r.ot."

Don't just take it for granted that everything will work out. The devil will take advantage of anything you leave to chance. God has a mouth; if you have ears He will talk to you. But you must seek His face.

James 4:2 says, "...Ye have not, because ye ask not." He also advised, "If any of you lack wisdom, let him ask of God, that giveth to all men liberally..." (James 1:5).

Many years ago while pastoring a church in Houston, Texas, I had a severe test of faith. My salary was $125 per week at that time. It was not bad for then. However, I faced a great dilemma: a 90-day note from the bank was due, and my source for handling it had fallen through. Suddenly, my automobile engine blew up with no warranty left. I felt like Elijah when the birds stopped feeding him and at the same time his brook dried up. I desperately needed $1,000 immediately, to cover the bank note and to replace my car engine. I panicked. I went to a loan shark (finance company), and applied for a $1,000 loan. I had borrowed from a finance company once before. But by the time I had finally paid all their charges, I promised myself that I would never do it again.

There I sat; the loan was approved and ready to sign. As I picked up the pen to sign the note, I heard inside me the word, **"Fool."**

I knew it was a warning, but I sat there thinking, *I don't have a choice.*

I started again to sign. And again the voice said, **"Fool,"** but this time the voice was stronger.

I just sat there. Finally I looked across the desk at the waiting loan officer and said, "I may be back tomorrow, but I am going to sleep on it."

However, that night I couldn't sleep. At two o'clock in the morning I was still walking the floor praying. What was I going to do? I pulled a Scripture promise card from my "promise box" which said the opposite of what my panic button told me: "Their strength is to sit still" (Isaiah 30:7).

I laid it aside and then drew several more, but nothing else spoke to me. I knew I should pay attention to that verse, so I looked up the chapter and its setting. When I finished reading the entire chapter, I laid my Bible down and made a decision: "I will not borrow the money." I didn't know what I *would* do; but I knew what I *wouldn't* do. I went to bed and to sleep.

At 8:00 the next morning, my phone rang. It was a lady in my church. She wanted my wife and me to come by as soon as we got out that morning. We went. She had sold some property, and said the Lord put it in her spirit to give us a check. It was a *cashier's check* for $1,000! I didn't have to pay that money back. What if I hadn't waited for God?

When your brook dries up, don't panic. Get guidance from God. "Trust in the Lord...Delight thyself also in Him; and He shall give thee the desires of thine heart" (Psalm 37:3-4).

## A Word from God

When his brook dried up, Elijah prayed. God spoke to him again saying, "Arise, get thee to Zarephath...and dwell there: behold, I have commanded a widow woman there to sustain thee" (I Kings 17:9). There it is again: "I have commanded." Before the brook dried up, God already had made arrangements to take care of Elijah.

In my case, the woman already had a check made out for me while I was sitting in the finance company worrying.

**DON'T PANIC!** Instead, pray and then listen for guidance. If your brook has dried up and you don't know of anything you have done to violate God's laws, then exercise your faith. Know that God already has made a way for you to escape the failure that looms ahead.

## Number Two: Don't Let the Devil Put You under Condemnation

The second thing you need to remember if your brook dries up is this: One of the first things Satan will tell you is, "This happened because of something you have done wrong."

If you have done something that you feel condemned in your conscience for, repent. God will forgive you. Then you must forgive yourself. After you repent, don't continue to labor under condemnation. You are forgiven.

Don't let the devil keep reminding you of your failures. He knows your *faith won't work* if you are in condemnation. Instead, remind him of what a failure he is. That will shut him down. Jesus said in John 14:27, "...Let not your heart be troubled, neither let it be afraid."

A condemning conscience fosters fear. This causes you to entertain thoughts like, *I guess I had it coming; I deserve it; the wild oats I've sown are catching up with me.* The devil will always remind you of how undeserving you are. But God has called you "worthy" through His Son, Jesus Christ. The only way goodness and mercy will follow you all the days of your life (Psalm 23:6) is to accept the position God has brought you into. Otherwise your faith can't function.

Don't let the devil bring you under condemnation. Remember, Paul said, "There is therefore now no condemnation to them which are in Christ Jesus, who walk not after the flesh, but after the Spirit" (Romans 8:1).

**Walk in the Spirit**
Paul further admonished, "If we live in the Spirit, let us also walk in the Spirit" (Galatians 5:25). This strongly implies that a person can indeed be in the Spirit life and not walk in its benefits. You are a conqueror only when you walk, as well as live, in the Spirit. John said, "Beloved, if our heart condemn us not, then have we confidence toward God" (I John 3:21).

Faith cannot survive in the presence of condemnation. Doubt your doubts and fear your fears, but never fear walking in faith. You can trust God. Remember, Elijah's brook dried up and the birds stopped coming as a result of his own faith ministry, not because of something he did wrong. *Your brook may have dried up because of something you did right.* Cast that in the devil's lap and see what he will do with it. That's resisting the devil, and I love to watch him flee.

Solomon observed, "The wicked flee when no man pursueth: but the righteous are bold as a lion" (Proverbs 28:1). You are the righteousness of God. The devil is the "wicked one." He will flee when you stand in faith and refuse condemnation.

# Number Three: Be Ready for Change

Now this is another thing to do if your brook dries up. I Kings 17:8-9 says, "The word of the Lord came unto him, saying, Arise, get thee to Zarephath, which belongeth to Zidon, and dwell there: behold, I have commanded a widow woman there to sustain thee." Human nature resents change. Moving from the known to experience the unknown and unexperienced is not something that we readily or easily do. Change is uncomfortable.

## Change Is Uncomfortable

Elijah was a man like we are. I can imagine his thoughts. "Zarephath? Zarephath? Why Zarephath? That's a Gentile town. My ministry is to the covenant people. Why would God want me to go there? I don't know anybody there! Why Zarephath?"

But he knew the voice of God. I can hear the turning of his mind now. "A widow there to sustain me?" The more he thought on it, the better it sounded. "A widow woman. Well all right! A rich widow. Apparently her husband died and left her rich. God has told her to feed me and give me a place to live. Okay, that sure beats this desert with no food or water."

## Our Presumptions

Haven't you ever tried to figure out how God was going to answer you? If you are human, you have. But it seldom works like you have it figured.

It is important to be ready for change. In following God, you will make many changes.

Sometimes a change in geographical location is necessary in order to move ahead with God. Many people have had to change doctrinally. Constant changes are necessary in our thinking, until we come to a knowledge of the fullness of God in Christ Jesus. Many people have had to change churches. We all have noticed changes in our relationships with people and friends. When we stop changing, we stop growing. Maybe this explains "growing pains." Change is uncomfortable but necessary for growth. **Your brook may have dried up to make you ready for that change.** Stay open to learning more truth. Buy books and tapes. If you think education is expensive, try ignorance. If Elijah hadn't been open to change and moving in faith he would have died in the desert. "My people are destroyed for lack of knowledge..." (Hosea 4:6). Be ready for change. When you are through changing, you are through!

Watch Elijah now as he makes his move. "Well, okay God, if Zarephath is it, then Zarephath here I come. Thank God for rich widows!" Notice that God never said she was rich. But, oh, how quickly we assume things. Elijah was a man just like we are, so wouldn't that be a normal thought.

## Appearances

By the time Elijah reached Zarephath he was dehydrated and hungry. As he approached the limits of the town, he began looking for a house that a rich widow would live in. But he was thirsty so he called to a servant woman who was gathering sticks for a fire, "Lady, would you please bring me a drink?"

"Why sure," replied the woman.

He lifted his gaze and began looking again. "Now, where does this rich widow live? Oh, Lord, I've come to Zarephath. Now where is she?" Can you imagine his shock when, as he turned to the servant woman, he heard a familiar voice inside say, "That's her"?

*What!! Oh, no!!* "Lady, bring me also a little cake."

"A little cake?" she shot back. "I don't have but one little cake, for myself and my little boy. And when that's gone, we are going to die. Haven't you heard? Are you a stranger around here? Some prophet stopped the rain two-and-one-half years ago and everybody's dying of hunger."

Elijah's face must have turned a little red. Suddenly it dawned on him. "So, I must live by faith again. This is the right town and the right woman, but she's a long way from being rich."

*Remember this:* **You will never be able to abandon living by faith,** no matter how prosperous you get in God.

# Number Four: Be Ready to Make a Sacrificial Donation to Someone Else's Need

This is the fourth thing you need to do if your brook dries up.

### The Widow Woman

In this fascinating story, there were two people whose "brooks" had dried up. Elijah's brook had dried up, as well as the widow woman's (her cruse of oil and meal barrel). Shift your thoughts now to the widow woman. She no doubt had been praying for a miracle, because God told Elijah He had "prepared a widow."

God speaks to people who pray, and whose thoughts are on Him.

God's command to this widow woman was to feed the man who stood before her. Elijah couldn't have come at a worse time, for she only had one meal left. You ask, *Would God actually do that?*

Yes, He actually asked that widow (with a starving child and no means of income) to give her last bite of food to an apparently prosperous preacher. Elijah wasn't skinny.

He had been eating twice a day while others had done without; hungry yes, but not skinny.

Why would God send a hungry preacher to a starving widow, and then ask her to feed her last bite of bread to the preacher instead of to her son? Can you imagine what the headlines of the *Zarephath News* would say if a reporter had been there? **"TRAVELING PREACHER BILKS WIDOW WOMAN AND SON OUT OF LAST BITE OF BREAD."**

This type of action can never match the comprehension of the natural mind. No wonder God says, "For my thoughts are not your thoughts, neither are your ways my ways..." (Isaiah 55:8). God's ways always revert back to seed-sowing —scattering to increase. They always require faith to overcome the world's system.

Elijah quickly gave her God's promise. "For thus saith the Lord God of Israel, The barrel of meal shall not waste, neither shall the cruse of oil fail, until the day that the Lord sendeth rain upon the earth" (I Kings 17:14). God is consistent about making and keeping His promises. But first, He must find someone who is consistent about believing and moving on them.

What Elijah did would be tantamount to any preacher who might ask a widow in church to give him her last five dollars. She probably would exclaim, "But preacher, that's all I have to buy a hamburger for my son and me to split after church. After that we won't have anything to eat."

Then he would say, "First give me that five dollars."

"Why? What are you going to do with it?"

"Buy me a hamburger after church," he might say.

How would you feel about a preacher who did that, if you didn't know the "rest of the story"? Now you can see why preachers who receive offerings get bad reviews. People don't know the rest of the story.

Elijah was a downright scoundrel until the widow looked back into her meal barrel. Then Elijah became her hero.

God never asks you to give to someone else's need at your own expense. He merely borrows from you and promises to repay with multiplied dividends (Proverbs 19:17).

God has two things in mind when He asks you to give:

1. The need and desire that you have been praying about
2. The need to which He has told you to give

Both Elijah and the widow woman had pressing needs. By using their faith, they each received a marvelous miracle.

Her brook had dried up, so she probably said, "I'm going to die anyway. But if I do what God says, maybe something will change." Since God had already spoken to her and prepared her for this (I Kings 17:9), she made her decision, "I'm going to do it."

There is always a release inside us when we exercise faith and move in obedience to God. An expectancy begins to build.

After giving the prophet her last meal, the widow just stood there watching as the man of God ate.

Now a cynic standing by, listening to their conversation and watching the prophet eat, might think, "Yeah, somebody's going to get blessed all right, and look who it will be."

But when that woman went inside her house, her shriek of ecstatic joy would fill any cynic with envy. "I wish God would do something like that for me," he might wish. But this doesn't come by wishing, it comes by moving in faith. So if your brook dries up, **be ready to make a sacrificial** donation to someone else's need.

Let us examine closely the blessing that followed the widow's act of faith and obedience. She lived on a continuous miraculous supply for a full year. No, she didn't get enough meal in her barrel to last a full year, instead she got a *daily refill* as she used the supply she had.

Now, look at the *kind* of supply she received. She fed herself and her little boy; and she was the sole sponsor of Elijah's ministry **during the famine.** When others couldn't even feed themselves, these three ate three meals a day. It was a miraculous *daily* supply in a time of famine.

### Daily Miracles Plus A Bonus

God opened the **windows of Heaven** to her. He gave her a daily miracle. But that is not the end of it. The widow's son became sick and died during that period. She was stricken with grief but because the widow was faithful to feed the prophet, he was there. The prophet took the boy up in his arms, carried him upstairs to his room and prayed over him till his life returned. If she hadn't obeyed God's command to give sacrificially, the man of God, Elijah, would not have been there when her boy died. She would have lost her son (I Kings 17:17-24).

Giving to God in faith comes back to you over and over again, when your brook dries up, be ready to **make a sacrificial contribution to someone else's need.**

# Number Five: Learn the Grace of Receiving

Now if your brook dries up, this is the last thing that I want to mention for you to do.

Shift your focus back to Elijah as he receives the food. He took it, thanked the widow and quietly began to eat.

There she and her little boy stood, watching as he ate their last meal. The little boy might very well have been crying, because children cry when they are hungry.

Elijah ate while they watched. Do you hate him? You might be thinking, *If he loved people, and if he genuinely was concerned about other peoples' needs, how could he do that? Any godly person would be concerned.*

You see, Elijah had learned the grace of receiving. For most people it is easier to learn the grace of *giving* than the grace of *receiving*. It feels good when we, as the strong, help the weak. This can actually stroke our pride. When we give, it places us above and not beneath. It makes us the head and not the tail (Deuteronomy 18:13).

However, when you receive, while it can bring a sense of relief, it also attacks your pride. You can't accomplish it yourself, and you can't make it without help! Independent-natured people, especially, have battles over this, saying things such as, "Oh no, I couldn't let you do that," or "No, I'm fine. I'll make it okay." The feeling is, *If I didn't do anything to deserve it, I won't take it.* That is pride taken to an extreme. We all should have pride in ourselves, but it needs to be kept in proper perspective.

If you are not willing to be a good receiver, you cannot help a giver receive his blessing. In short, the giver can't be blessed if there are no receivers.

Very often, the person who has learned the grace of receiving must encourage the giver to exercise his faith. Is it a lack of concern for others that allows the receiver to do this? Is it a selfish attitude to encourage others to give to your need? No.

Obviously, this grace of receiving goes much deeper. To help you understand this, let's look at God as the receiver and at us as the givers. It doesn't void love to ask someone to give. If it did, then God (Who is love) couldn't require us to give Him our lives. Neither could He be aggressive about commanding us to give Him 10% of all our increase. We know that God is a good receiver. But why does He frequently ask us to give to Him? Why do preachers also ask us to give? What is it? **It is a personal revelation of understanding about the cycle of things.**

It is true that some dishonest receivers may use this method to pad their own interests with little regard to the donors. However, this is not what happens in the heart of the Spirit-led child of God who encourages others to give to his cause. He is absolutely convinced that God cannot lie. He KNOWS that the donor is going to receive from God a full supply, according to the donor's measure of giving.

Therefore, the Spirit-led child subjects himself to the ridicule of on-lookers who do not understand or appreciate this principle.

You cannot see God's miracles until you move in His principles. When you do this, you go beyond the natural laws to activate the spiritual laws. Then you see Heaven's order of things override the world's order of things.

- It is faith overpowering doubt.
- It is worry overcome by trust.
- It is taking nothing and converting it into something.
- It is what turns failure into success.

When it is your turn to receive, don't put up your palms and refuse. Overpower that impulse to salvage your pride. Receive the blessing with thanksgiving, and open the door for the other person to be blessed. It is the Father's good pleasure to give His children good things. When you refuse to receive, you hinder God from His enjoyment, stop the donor from being blessed, and remain in your distressing lifestyle. All this, just because you want to protect your pride.

Is it any wonder that Scripture warns, "Pride goeth before destruction, and an haughty spirit before a fall" (Proverbs 16:18).

When you think of Elijah eating that cake in front of the starving widow and her little boy, you are certainly brought to a point of meditation.

God said he was going to have a "peculiar people." Once you know Him, you certainly will not think in typical human patterns. It is part of "putting on the mind of Christ."

If you do not accept the grace of receiving, you will never be able to walk in God's promise of abundance. How can He give you more, if you don't have the capacity to receive it?

Meditate on Proverbs 30 which tells of King Agur who had not learned the grace of receiving. He even prayed for God *not* to give him riches. His vision for the salvation of the lost was obviously non-existent.

We can never have the abundance we need to reach the world with the Gospel, until we learn the grace of receiving. Don't limit God.

When your brook dries up, start looking for a miracle supply. Follow God's guidance with expectation. Then when it comes, be ready to receive; but watch out that pride doesn't get in your way. God's way may be humbling, but "...He that humbleth himself shall be exalted" (Luke 14:11). You can start giving again as soon as you have something to give.

Sometimes these experiences are necessary to teach us to be good givers. Times of humiliation can create in us an appreciation toward giving, and an understanding of what it means to be a good giver. Some people never become good givers until they experience having to be helped. It teaches them something about giving that they cannot learn any other way.

As soon as Elijah finished his meal, he instructed the woman, "Now go to the meal barrel and prepare a cake for you and the boy." No doubt there was indescribable joy in his heart when he heard the woman's shriek of excitement and saw her dancing and praising God.

If you want to be a blessing to others and glorify God Almighty, you must learn the grace of receiving.

## Summary

Let this chapter and its message **inspire** you. Maybe you *know* you are in the will of God, yet you are facing challenges that *definitely* seem to be "out of order!" There you are, more than likely, feeling just like the prophet Elijah, whose story we have just examined in detail. Like him, you might be feeling totally abandoned in the "drought" of your circumstances. Like him, you are crying out to God.

Remember, **don't panic!** God most assuredly is preparing today for your victory tomorrow. You can stake your bottom dollar that His solution is better and more rewarding than you can imagine. Be convinced that you are moving toward an even *greater* opportunity to be blessed and to be a blessing.

Pray and seek His face. Don't hinder God. **Accept** this situation as a *challenge* to change directions.

Don't let the enemy tell you that you are a failure at this vulnerable time! I feel it is important to re-emphasize Romans 8:1. "There is therefore now *no* condemnation to them which are in Christ Jesus...."

NEVER abandon your stand of faith. Exercise it by finding a way to give to *someone else's* need...this is guaranteed to build a sense of *expectancy* into your circumstances. It's an excellent way to by-pass the natural laws and surge ahead into *God's* order of things...and the **certainty** of your miracle. Glory to God!

As long as the widow woman held onto her little bit, she expected to die. As soon as she released it to God, she began to expect a miracle.

God said He would not cut us short of our expectations. Meditate on it.

# 12

# The Secret
# to Obtaining Scriptural Wealth

As I begin this chapter, I would like you to realize that to obtain the secret of wealth you must step over an important line. Remember:

> But thou shalt remember the Lord thy God: for it is he that giveth thee *power to get wealth,* that he may establish his covenant which he sware unto thy fathers, as it is this day.
>
> Deuteronomy 8:18

Notice here that God didn't say He gives us *wealth,* but the *"POWER to get wealth."* **This secret power is in our covenant with God.** To better understand, let's consider Samson, a man who had a covenant with God for physical power (Judges 13-16, paraphrased).

## Samson's Secret

"Oh, Samson," begged Delilah, the woman he loved, "tell me wherein thy great strength lies." Samson toyed with her and tantalized her with false solutions to discover his supernatural strength. She then revealed these "solutions" to Israel's captors, the Philistines. But each time when the Philistines trapped Samson according to Delilah's instructions, Samson rose up and destroyed many of them.

The great power was in him to rise above every obstacle, no matter what the Philistines did to bring him down. No matter how great the army or tools they used against Samson, nothing could stop him, because he did not abandon the source of his strength. *He had a secret* **that caused him to succeed at everything he put his hands to.** He had no fear of failure.

When a lion came out to stop Samson's progress and to devour him, he slew the beast with his bare hands. Samson had POWER because he had a secret. Later he returned to the lion's carcass and drew honey for his sustenance, out of what was meant to kill him. That lion would have killed anyone else, but Samson had a secret. He had supernatural power because of this secret. "...Out of the eater came forth meat, and out of the strong came forth sweetness" (Judges 14:14). What was designed against him was reversed to be a blessing.

Nothing could stop Samson, not even the gates of the city. Once, he pulled them from their mighty hinges and carried them to the top of the hill.

"Oh, Samson," Delilah pleaded again and again, "tell me wherein thy great strength lies." No weapon formed against him could prosper. (This is true for you, too!)

> **No weapon that is formed against thee shall prosper; and every tongue that shall rise against thee in judgment thou shalt condemn. This is the heritage of the servants of the Lord, and their righteousness is of me, saith the Lord.**
> **Isaiah 54:17**

Samson had a secret. However because of Delilah's continuous pressure on him, he eventually gave in and revealed his secret to her:

> ...There hath not come a razor upon mine head; for I have been a Nazarite unto God from my mother's womb: if I be shaven, then my strength will go from me, and I shall become weak, and be like any other man.
>
> **Judges 16:17**

Samson's secret was in his covenant with his God. You see, God had chosen Samson to covenant with Him for life to deliver Israel from the Philistines (Judges 13:1-7).

After Samson revealed his secret, Delilah had Samson's hair shaved off. Because this symbolized a broken covenant with God, Samson's strength was gone. When the Philistines seized him, they overpowered him and gouged out his eyes.

## Never Forsake Your Faith Covenant

**When Samson forsook his covenant with God, he lost his power and became as any other man.**

In total blindness he was made to push the "grinding wheel" of the Philistines' financial system. When his hair grew out (the covenant was restored), his power returned. Read about it in the Bible (Judges 16:21-31).

Now, **how does this apply to our finances?**

## We Have a Secret

As we studied in an earlier chapter, Jesus told the people and His disciples the parable of the sower and the various types of ground that the seed fell into (Matthew 13).

> And the disciples came, and said unto him, Why
> speakest thou unto them in parables?
> **Matthew 13:10**

Look closely at Jesus' answer:

> ...Because it is *given unto you to know the mysteries*
> *[secrets] of the kingdom of heaven,* but to them it is not given.
> **Matthew 13:11**

Consider what God says in Proverbs 3:32.

> For the froward [ungodly and disobedient] is abomi-
> nation to the Lord: but his *secret is with the righteous.*
> **Proverbs 3:32**

We, God's covenant children, have a secret which is
made available to everyone, because it is clearly stated in
the Bible. However, it is only understood by those who will
switch from walking by sight to walking by faith. **The
secret, like Samson's riddle, is a mystery to the ungodly,
but known and understood by those who have the
revelation.**

> ...If thou wilt...apply thine heart to understanding;
> Yea, if thou criest after knowledge...seekest [for] her as
> silver, and searchest for her as for HID TREASURES; Then
> shalt thou understand...and find the knowledge of God.
> **Proverbs 2:1-5**

> Wilt thou set thine eyes upon that which is not? for
> riches [that is wealth gained aside from that acquired through

scriptural procedures] certainly make themselves wings;
they fly away as an eagle toward heaven.

Proverbs 23:5

# The Lottery

The lottery (riches gotten hastily) often corrupts its
recipient because it is not generated through proper principles and channels. Therefore, the understanding of how to
handle it is not equal to the weight and responsibility of it.
It will fly away, bringing instead hurt or destruction.

> **Wealth gotten by vanity shall be diminished: but he
> that gathereth by labour shall increase.**

Proverbs 13:11

# The Laws of Heaven

We have all heard it said, "When all else fails, read the
instructions." When you press in to learn and practice God's
laws, it will affect every area of your life, including your
finances. Jesus talked about money more than any other
Bible personality. He described how the laws of Heaven
work in relation to finances. Jesus began to reveal the secret:

> **For whosoever hath, to him shall be given, and he shall
> have more abundance: but whosoever hath not, from him
> shall be taken away even that he hath.**

Matthew 13:12

Jesus illustrated this law in the parable of the pounds,
recorded in Luke 19:12-26. (Similarly, the parable of the
talents is found in Matthew 25:14-30.) Before going on a

journey, a nobleman gave each of his ten servants one pound. Upon his return, the nobleman demanded a tally of the servants' activities with his money.

The first man had taken his pound and developed ten. Likewise the second man had taken his pound and developed five. But the third man, returning his one pound said:

> Here is thy pound, which I have kept laid up in a napkin: For I feared....
>
> Luke 19:20-21

The nobleman replied:

> ...Take from him the pound, and give it to him that hath ten pounds.
>
> Luke 19:24

Notice he didn't give it to the one who had five, but to the *one who had developed the most.* Everyone was shocked (verse 25).

This is the principle by which Heaven judges our financial procedures. It is also Heaven's reward system.

> ...For with the same measure that ye mete withal it shall be measured to you again.
>
> Luke 6:38

The person who operates best in this system will eventually have the possessions of those who live in fear.

## A New Principle

When Jesus taught this principle in Matthew 13:12—

that whoever has, to him more abundance will be given—He was the first to ever teach it (as declared in verse 17). The disciples did not understand this principle when Jesus told the parable of the pounds. Luke 19:25 tells us that the people were shocked at this teaching. They protested in amazement:

> ...[But] Lord, he hath ten pounds.
>
> **Luke 19:25**

Why, they wondered, would Jesus say that to those who have, more will be given; and those who don't have much, what little they *do* have will be taken from them and given to the one who has the most?

## Jesus Taught Capitalism

Even today many Christians do not understand it, but this is the way capitalistic systems function. Our godly forefathers understood it and started our government that way. Paul also understood it when he said, "...If any would not work, neither should he eat" (II Thessalonians 3:10).

I know the disciples and the people didn't understand the function of this principle because of what they did in Acts 4.

## The Disciples Missed the Principle (Secret)

Acts 4 describes how the people, in their enthusiasm, began selling their properties and putting everything in the disciples' hands. These Christians began living according to basic communistic principles. Everybody "had all things common" (Acts 4:32). Because of this unscriptural pattern of handling finances, the sin of Ananias and Sapphira was set up. A curse fell on them and they died for lying about their financial dealings (Acts 5:1-10).

These early Christians were dangerously close to becoming a cult. The disciples were in charge of everyone's money, "...and they distributed to each as anyone had need" (Acts 4:35, NKJV). This is how communism operates.

If the disciples had understood Jesus' teaching in Matthew 13:12 they would not have cooperated in this. Nowhere does the Scripture say that the Holy Ghost told the people to bring all their money and have all things common. If He had, He would have been in disagreement with Jesus' teaching in Matthew 13:12, which is how the capitalistic system operates. (Remember, the person who operates best in this system will eventually have the possessions of those who live in fear.) The Spirit and the Word always agree. If the Holy Ghost had initiated it, He would have perpetuated it, but we don't follow that pattern in our churches today.

## Trusting God with Money

The Bible does encourage us to give our finances and possessions to the kingdom's work, but not to a communistic system of living. When we give to God's kingdom, we will receive a return.

When is this return supposed to come to pass? Consider Mark 10:29-30. In this passage, Jesus explained what happens when a man leaves (or invests) all he has—houses, lands, family, etc.—for Jesus' and the Gospel's sake:

> ...There is no man that hath left house, or brethren, or sisters, or father, or mother, or wife, or children, or lands, for my sake, and the gospel's,

> But he shall receive [generate] an hundredfold [spiritual, physical and material blessings], *now [Now! Now! Now!] in this time*...and in the world to come eternal life.
>
> Mark 10:29–30

The return comes *both now, while you are alive* on earth, *and in Heaven*. It is an investment.

This immediately launches the question: How do I go about making this investment?

# Do You Trust God?

Let me first point out that you alone can determine if you can trust God with your money, as much as you trust Him with your soul. **Do you believe that you can trust God to keep you in this life, as much as you trust Him to take care of you when you die?** Once you determine this, then you are prepared to accept His teachings on how and where to invest your money.

# Be Comfortable with Money

In Luke 16:9 Jesus told us to make friends with money, so that when you fail (in your efforts to publish the Gospel), money will redeem you from failure.

# How Do You Associate?

- If you think like the poor, you'll be poor.
- If you talk like the poor, you'll be poor.
- If you live among the poor, you'll be poor.

We rise or fall to the level of our associations. According to the Word of God, poverty is a curse. We must change our *thinking*, before *things* can change.

# Proportionately Multiplied Rewards

In the parable of the pounds (Luke 19:12-26), the first fellow returned his pound with a gain of ten pounds. For this, he earned the reward of being over ten cities (verse 17). The second fellow gained five pounds for his pound, and was given the reward of being over five cities (verse 19). Notice that the reward was equal to his faith accomplishments. However, the next fellow did not invest his pound, because he was afraid (verses 20–21). Because of this, his one pound was taken from him, and given to the fellow with ten pounds. This fellow was afraid to invest, because he was afraid of losing what he had. Thus, he lost it all.

## The Fear Factor

Notice here that fear was the problem. Today, when people fail to tithe and give liberally, it isn't because of ignorance that it takes money to run God's work; they are fully aware of this fact. It isn't necessarily a lack of love for God. The problem is that they have not overcome fear. In short, they simply don't trust God. They fear losing what little they *do* have. And the thing they fear will come upon them (Job 3:25).

In this story of the pounds, the fearful man lost what he had been given, and it went to the person who best operated the investment principles. Jesus wants us to increase. The better we work His system, the more pleased He is.

In Matthew 6:31–34 Jesus told the people not to worry about tomorrow, because God knew what they needed. But how can we get past worry and the fear of not making it, as generated by TV and other media? How can we begin believing that we don't have to retire in poverty?

When a journalist asked industrialist Armand Hammer how he had made it so big (his 747 jet was like a loaded RV, with gold faucets, king-size beds, etc.), he said he attributed his success to the fact that he was never afraid to turn loose of a dollar.

## Faith to Let Go

It takes faith to let go of your money. You must be ready to shift from **living by sight** to **living by faith.** After you make this change, you will always be tempted to stray from faith. Negative appearances may arise. But remember the question, *Do you trust God?*

## Temporary Versus Eternal

It is amazing, exhausting and exasperating to think of how many people trust God with their ETERNAL, UNSEEN SOULS compared to how few of those same people trust Him with their MONEY. We trust God with *a soul we haven't seen,* to save us from *a Hell we haven't seen,* and to take us to *a Heaven we haven't seen.* Yet we struggle over trusting Him with our *money—which we CAN see—*in this fleeting and temporary life. Why can we only trust God with the UN-SEEN, but not the SEEN?

## You Trusted Him with Your Soul

You did what God told you to do in order to get saved. You trusted Him with your soul, so you don't have to pray for salvation anymore. You now have confidence in Him to supply you with eternal life. The same will be true about your money, when you learn to do with your investments what God has told you to do.

## Praying for Money

I am fully convinced that **if we do what God has told us to do with our money, we will not have to pray for money anymore.** I don't mean to imply that all faith battles in this area will stop, but the money will be there when needed. It will come in "due season" by faith.

Now let's proceed. What is the big secret to obtaining wealth?

## Samson's Secret—Our Secret

With Samson it was simple, never cut his hair or drink wine. This was called a Nazarite's vow. It was a covenant with God. Samson functioned in the supernatural as long as he maintained these qualifications and fulfilled his part of the covenant. God's promise to all His children is this:

> **When the world is in famine, my children shall be fed.**
> **Psalm 37:19, paraphrased**

*That is supernatural.*
Paul admonished:

**If we live in the Spirit, let us also walk in the Spirit.**
**Galatians 5:25**

You can be in the benefits (where they are), yet miss **walking** (participating) in the benefits. Are you ready for Jesus' instructions? Here they are:

**Lay not up for yourselves treasures upon EARTH, where moth and rust doth corrupt, and where thieves break through and steal.**

**But lay up for yourselves treasures in HEAVEN, where neither moth nor rust doth corrupt, and where thieves do not break through nor steal.**
**Matthew 6:19-20**

I don't understand Jesus to be saying that it is a sin to invest in earthly commodities, but that it simply is not a sure thing or a no-risk investment. On earth, the thief of inflation has eroded for many people the value of their lifetime savings. Earthly investments are risky.

## The World's System

Recently I heard a senator say that by the year 2000 there would be no Social Security. Today, 90% of all retirees retire below the poverty level. The government and the world system cannot supply us. The Social Security system is failing; no man or committee can fix the problem. There is no security in this world's system.

- Fire can consume any investment on earth
- Banks fail
- Insurance companies collapse

- High-dollar shares can reverse overnight
- Human thieves are increasing

Both white-collar thieves and street hoodlums are increasing. Nothing on earth is really secure. One major sickness can wipe out a lifetime of savings and leave you in abject poverty. Everyone knows this; no one will argue about it.

However, the thought remains: it's the best you can do. So, you do all you can and just hope for the best. After all, that is all a person can do if that is all he knows. This is typical thinking.

But remember, we are not "as others which have no hope" (I Thessalonians 4:13).

We are IN this world, but we are not OF this world. In Matthew 6:24-33, Jesus tells us not to worry about food, clothes or drink. The Gentiles (ungodly, unregenerate, non-covenant people) seek after these things. But we are not to seek these things. We are not to put our affection on the things here on earth.

What about these things? Jesus said that our Heavenly Father knows our need for these things. However, He instructed that we are to seek God first, and all the things we need will come from Him.

## Two Systems

In Matthew 13 Jesus said that there are two systems: God's and the world's. Then He told us how to function supernaturally in this world, by committing to God our interests. Only in this way will we get His work done.

# God First

When we put first things first (God's work), the things we need will come. Then the ungodly will say:

> ...Let us go with you, because we have heard that God is with you.
>
> **Zechariah 8:23 (NIV)**

They will see the blessing of God on your life, and they will want it in their lives, especially in a bad economy.

Yes, *we can live in this earthly economy, according to Heaven's economy.*

> **But my God [your God] shall supply all your need** *according to his riches in glory by Christ Jesus.*
>
> **Philippians 4:19**

# Material Things

Having *things* is not most important. But if you delight yourself in God, meditate in His Word and do it, these good gifts will come to you. God's investment program will cause you—even in old age—to be "fat and flourishing" (Psalm 92:14). Remember, God's system declares:

> **Surely goodness and mercy shall follow me** *all the days of my life....*
>
> **Psalm 23:6**

Only two things can stop your flow of blessing:

1. You either don't *know* what to do.
2. Or you know what to do, but you *refuse* to do it.

In this book, I have endeavored to show you what to do to be blessed. Now, you *know* what to do. It's your decision to do it.

## True Security

God's financial plan is a NO-RISK investment program. It certainly is not a sin to take advantage of a good investment opportunity in some natural or temporal commodity. However, the deceit is in believing that your security lies in reserve funds and excessive net worth. If your total motivation for all you do is based on how it will affect your money, that is where your sense of security is. If your affection is on "things below," it is because you have not "died and risen with the Lord." It is because you have not abandoned your trust in the earthly system and adopted God's system. (See Colossians 3.)

## The Realm of Faith

> Set your affection on *things above,* and not on *things on the earth.*
>
> **Colossians 3:2**

Cross over the line. You not only need to be saved in your soul and trust God with your eternity, but you need to renew your mind.

> And be not conformed to this world: but be ye trans-

formed by the renewing of your mind, that ye may prove
what is that good, and acceptable, and perfect, will of God.
**Romans 12:2**

**Learn now to trust God with your money.** You can
change your present financial status by crossing over the
line. Trust His financial system, and let your thinking fall
into another realm—the realm of faith.

## Summary

Cross over the line by moving away from the **carnal**
procedures that the world functions in—that is, trusting in
earthly investments, which are certain to be risky—and
moving into the **faith** realm. This brings you into the supernatural life, which allows you to walk in **the power to get
wealth.**

This is the secret.

God gives us power to get wealth, so he can establish
His covenant. Even God needs money, or He wouldn't have
taken the wealth of the ungodly and given it to the righteous. Since Christians are the only ones who care about
getting His business done on earth, He wants to give us the
power to get wealth so we can do His work.

With this power you will become a Samson who causes
others to look at you and call you blessed. You will succeed
while others fail. You will keep going UP while others are
going UNDER. You will become a mystery to your peers. In
Malachi 3:12, God says that others will observe you and call
you blessed, and you will have a **"delightsome"** lifestyle.
Then, you can lead them to Jesus.

To do this, you must decide to put His concerns and
interests first. TRUST HIM. Invest according to His directions and instructions. **Promote *His* cause first with your**

**best investment money. Then watch for your increase.** God will cause some people to give increase to you voluntarily and some to give involuntarily. Nevertheless, while others lose because they are holding and holding, you will increase because you are scattering and scattering.

Now, consider how to do this in the next and final chapter.

# 13

# God's Plan for Old Age

Today, there is great concern about financial security in old age. As mentioned in the previous chapter, recently I heard a senator say that by the year 2000 there would be no Social Security. Now, 90% of all retirees retire below the poverty level.

God has a better plan for old age. His social security system will never fail you. Read what He promises for YOUR retirement if you are His child:

> The righteous shall flourish like the palm tree: he shall grow like a cedar in Lebanon.
>
> Those that be planted in the house of the Lord shall flourish in the courts of our God.
>
> They shall still bring forth fruit in old age; they shall be fat and flourishing;
>
> To shew that the Lord is upright: he is my rock, and there is no unrighteousness in him.
>
> Psalm 92:12-15

When you cross over from the natural to the realm of faith, you will trust this procedure.

Remember from the previous chapter of this book that Jesus said:

> But *lay up for yourselves treasures in heaven* where neither moth nor rust doth corrupt, and where thieves do not break through nor steal.
>
> **Matthew 6:20**

Notice that Jesus' concern in this teaching is for the investor's security. He is concerned that you don't lose your investment. He is teaching you to lay up for yourself—not on earth, but in Heaven—lest you lose it. You won't have any needs in Heaven, but what you put into Heaven will supply your needs on earth.

> But my God shall supply all your need according to his riches in glory by Christ Jesus.
>
> **Philippians 4:19**

Even in "old age," you will be "fat and flourishing" (Psalm 92:14).

## God's Social Security Program

"Lay up for yourself" is terminology obviously describing an investment, but an investment for whom? *Yourself!* "Lay up for *yourselves* treasures in heaven."

## How It Works

Now, how do you do that? Scripture explains it very clearly. Let's look at Philippians 4:15-19.

> Now ye Philippians know also, that in the beginning of the gospel, when I departed from Macedonia, no church communicated with me as concerning giving and receiving, but ye only.
>
> For even in Thessalonica ye sent once and again unto my necessity.
>
> Not because I desire a gift: but I desire fruit that may *abound to your account.*
>
> But I have all, and abound: I am full, having received of Epaphroditus the things which were sent from you, an odour of a sweet smell, a sacrifice acceptable, wellpleasing to God.
>
> But my God shall supply all your need according to his riches in glory by Christ Jesus.
>
> Philippians 4:15-19

Paul, a missionary to Thessalonica, wrote this letter of approval to the Christians in Philippi. In this letter he spoke of "giving and receiving." He commended them for their repetition in supplying the needs of his missionary endeavors. Because of their continuance in this, he could say: "But I have all, and abound: I am full...."

In verse 17, Paul made a very profound statement. He told the Philippians that their giving of support in extending the Gospel was fruit that may abound to **their account.**

## Heaven's Treasurer—Keeper of Accounts

Where was their account? Obviously Paul meant **in Heaven.** In the parable of the pounds (from Luke 19) that we talked about earlier in the previous chapter, the nobleman scolded the man who feared to invest the money given to him and said, "Wherefore did you not put my money in the bank, so that on my return I might have collected my own with usury [interest]" (verse 23, paraphrased). Notice in Jesus' parable that the nobleman referred to *the* bank not *a* bank. Evidently Jesus has confidence in a particular bank. As soon as you begin to tithe and give to support God's work, you set up your account in Heaven's bank. An account is set up for deposits *and* withdrawals.

Who keeps these accounts? Heaven's Treasurer. Who is that? JESUS! Jesus is Heaven's Treasurer and our great High Priest.

> **And here men that die receive tithes; but there [in Heaven] he [Jesus] receiveth them, of whom it is witnessed that he liveth.**
>
> **Hebrews 7:8**

- Abraham paid tithes to Melchizedek, a high priest and king of Salem.

But we have a better priesthood.

- Jesus Christ is the High Priest of a better covenant. Today, we give our tithes and offerings to men who are chosen of God to carry on Jesus' ministry here on earth.

But the truth is **the Lord Jesus is the One we pay our tithes to.** Remember:

> **Whatsoever ye do, do it heartily, *as to the Lord,* and not unto men.**
>
> **Colossians 3:23**

Jesus is sitting at the right hand of the Father, making intercession for the saints and keeping books on our tithes and offerings. He told us that Heaven's supply is available to us in direct proportion to our investment (Luke 6:38).

## God Is the President of Heaven's Bank

Every Christian has an account in Heaven, and there are no mistakes in Jesus' bookkeeping. **God protects your investment with His integrity.** Without integrity, God would not be God. Heaven and earth will fail before God's Word can fail. God is God because He can be trusted. Not a jot or a tittle of His Word has ever failed. *That is a true NO-RISK investment.*

## NO-RISK Investment

Remember, your investment is with God, not necessarily in a particular ministry. If the ministry you invested in defaults in some way, the minister will give an account to the Lord for the way his ministry spent, used or abused God's money. But this has NO AFFECT on your investment plan. You did it as unto the Lord, and the Lord promised He would repay. "I will repay" saith the Lord (Luke 10:35). God will back up your investment with His own integrity. You don't have to worry. Again, it is a NO-RISK investment.

## Investment Returns

Now consider the level of return on this kind of investment:

> **It shall be given unto you; good measure, pressed down, and shaken together, and running over....**
> **Luke 6:38**

God also promises to make you a lender so you will not have to borrow (Deuteronomy 28:12). This means that you will have more than enough for your own maintenance. You also will have excess to help others. He will make you to be **the strong supporting the weak,** instead of **the weak supported by the strong.**

## How Do We Make Our Deposits?

You already know what *tithe* means? "One-tenth." The first tenth of all our increase is God's money to begin with. Our tithe cannot be counted as an investment. It is not ours to control or to give. The tithe is called "holy unto the Lord" (Leviticus 27:30). Holy money! By tithing we simply are not stealing God's money. He calls it "robbery" when we don't give it to Him (Malachi 3:8).

> **Will a man rob God? Yet ye have robbed me. But ye say, Wherein have we robbed thee? In tithes and offerings.**
> **Malachi 3:8**

> **It is a snare to the man who devoureth that which is holy....**
> **Proverbs 20:25**

Now, I want you to ponder something with me carefully. When you tithe, are you giving God *your* money or *His* money?? God views the tithe—10% of your earnings—as *His* money. Therefore, you still have 100%, not 90%, of *your* money after you tithe. Do you agree? Now, let's discuss offerings. Would you agree that an offering must come out of *your* money after you give to God *His* money (the tithe)?

## God's Money Versus Our Money

Think with me here: when you tithe, you are being a good steward of *God's* money by putting it where He instructed—"the storehouse" (Malachi 3:10).

Read Malachi 3:10–11. Notice that there are two separate blessings mentioned for the tither or giver:

> Bring ye all the tithes into the storehouse, that there may be meat in mine house, and prove me now herewith, saith the Lord of hosts, if I will not open you the windows of heaven, and *pour you out a blessing, that there shall not be room enough to receive it.*
>
> And I will *rebuke the devourer for your sakes,* and he shall not destroy the fruits of your ground; neither shall your vine cast her fruit before the time in the field, saith the Lord of hosts.
>
> Malachi 3:10–11

In these verses, God says He will "...pour you out a blessing, that there shall not be room enough to receive it" and "...rebuke the devourer for your sakes." God even promises to stop your enemies (the devourer) from stealing from you!

Question: If you went to work for a farmer and sowed seed in his fields all day, you would be a seed sower, wouldn't you? But the farmer would get the harvest, wouldn't he? Why? Because he owned the seed! He merely paid you wages for sowing *his* seed. That is what happens when you sow God's seed (the tithe) for Him. He pays you wages for being a good steward of *His* seed. He says in effect, "If you don't steal My money, I won't let the devil steal your money." He rebukes the devourer for your sake. That's the blessing that comes from *tithing.*

If you want the additional "windows–in–Heaven" blessing poured out till you don't have room to receive it, then you must give *offerings* from *your* money. You must *own* the seed. Get your own plot of ground, so to speak—such as a missions project—and sow your seed liberally. Give offerings to that work out of your money. Then, you will get your *own* harvest from your *own* seed.

Your cup will run over (excess) all the days of your life, if you practice **giving your seed** liberally all the days of your life.

Everything we are, have and own belongs to God anyway. We are simply stewards of His belongings—even the remaining money, after the tithe. But He leaves it to our discretion to do with the remaining portion as we choose, unless He puts before us an amount of money or an item in our possession as a requested offering.

## Robbing God of an Offering

You are robbing God, if He speaks to you to give an amount of money and you do not obey, or if He puts an item in your spirit to give and you refuse. Now you know how you can rob God of an offering. We are to be led by the Spirit in our giving. Be sure to be sensitive to that voice.

However, unless God puts a specific figure in your heart to give, you simply can pick a figure of your own to invest. Either way He counts your offerings, above the tithe, as investments.

- The offering generates a harvest.
- Obedience in tithing keeps the curse off YOUR money.

# Loaning Money to God

The real truth about giving to support God's interests is that God views it as a loan. This He clearly states in His Word.

**He that hath pity upon the poor lendeth unto the Lord; and that which he hath given will he pay him again.**
**Proverbs 19:17**

**He that hath a bountiful eye shall be blessed; for he giveth of his bread to the poor.**
**Proverbs 22:9**

**He that giveth unto the poor shall not lack....**
**Proverbs 28:27**

**He that by usury and unjust gain increaseth his substance, he shall gather it for him that will pity the poor.**
**Proverbs 28:8**

Considering the verses previously mentioned, *giving* your money is viewed by God the Father and the Lord Jesus Christ as a loan or investment. The *tithe* is not, because it isn't your money.

Many people today spend lots of money going to seminars on finance, but the best information is right here in the Bible: helping the poor.

# Giving to the Poor Is an Investment

One may ask, "Is it right to give money to the poor as an investment?"

If you loan money to God, don't you think He will pay it back? You trust Him with your soul. Here, the Bible is telling you how to get God in debt to you.

But you say, "What can the poor do for me?" Nothing. You gave it to the *poor*, but it was a loan to *God*.

Nowadays, when we invest, we want to get a contract signed. We have learned that we cannot trust people. A handshake used to be all that was needed. No more. Today, you must sign a contract. I saw a sign in the window of a business: "In God we trust, all others pay cash." God can be trusted.

Investing in the poor is how you invest money without taking a loss. Then you can retire above the poverty level. The more you invest in God's work (lend to Him), the better you work His system, the more you gain so you can again invest in His work.

## Who Are the Poor?

Now, before we continue, we need to know the answer to this question: Who are the poor? God instructs us to give to the poor, but who are the poor? I have pointed out earlier in this book that God's thoughts and our thoughts are usually far apart. What counts are *His* views on who the poor are. In order to deposit into His bank we need to follow His deposit instructions.

Observe now whom God calls poor:

> Because thou sayest, I am rich, and increased with goods, and have need of nothing; and knowest not that thou art wretched, and miserable, and poor, and blind, and naked.
>
> **Revelation 3:17**

In this verse, God is speaking to the church in Laodicea.

- Listen to how *they* think of themselves: "...I am rich, and increased with goods, and have need of nothing...."
- Now look at how *God* thinks of them: "...knowest not that thou art wretched, and miserable, and **poor,** and blind, and naked."

The poor, according to Jesus (these are *His* words), are those who are not educated according to God's ways, methods and provisions. When *we* speak of the poor, we think of people in poverty *financially.* But *God* is thinking of people who are poor *spiritually.* Even though they may live in palaces, they are poor if they are not saved and spiritually developed. The Laodiceans said they were rich, but God said they were poor. God said to the church in Smyrna (Revelation 2:8-9), you say you are poor, "but thou art rich...." We must view things the way God does.

## Missions—Reaching the Poor

According to God, investing to reach the lost and spiritually uneducated is covered as giving to the poor. When you give as a partner to a ministry which is reaching the unreached and telling the untold, you are giving to the poor. Giving in this manner (as well as personally spreading the Good News) is "laying up treasures in Heaven" for yourself.

## The Head—Not the Tail

Now, I want to point out something that God promised to His covenant people in Deuteronomy 28:2-13. He summarized the abundant lifestyle they would have:

> The Lord shall open unto thee *his good treasure* [Heaven's provision]...to bless all the work of thine hand: and thou shalt lend...and thou shalt not borrow.
>
> And the Lord shall make thee *the head, and not the tail;* and thou shalt be above only, and thou shalt not be beneath....
>
> Deuteronomy 28:12-13

Now, carefully meditate on the following verse.

> The rich ruleth over the poor, and the borrower is servant to the lender.
>
> Proverbs 22:7

According to this verse in Proverbs, **you will only become the head instead of the tail when you become a lender instead of a borrower.** Loan it to God—He will make you fat.

## Cross over the Line

The weak are often categorized as poor—not rich—having no voice, no authority, no leadership, no respect, and no honor. Jesus said, "...You have the poor with you always..." (Matthew 26:11, NKJV), but that is not God's will.

God's promise of ascendancy in this life is predicated on whether you are the LENDER instead of the BORROWER. Face the facts. Until you gain control in the financial realm, you will not realize the fulfillment of God's promise in Deuteronomy 8.

But thou shalt remember the Lord thy God: for it is he that giveth thee power to get wealth, that he may establish his covenant which he sware unto thy fathers, as it is this day.

**Deuteronomy 8:18**

## Summary

You can enjoy GOD'S plan of security! When you walk by faith in HIS supernatural power, He will take care of you. He will provide for you when the world's economy is falling apart (when the famine is on). You can choose to live in Heaven's economy ON EARTH. When you do this, you will have clothes, be fed and filled, and praise God—even in OLD AGE! You will defy the world's system and cause your latter years to be fruit-bearing ones.

In I Kings 17:6 God caused the ravens to bring meat and food to Elijah during the famine. Ravens don't kill. God sent the ravens to get the food for the prophet from the only person who had food—King Ahab. Elijah ate the dainties of the *king's table*. Remember, there was a famine, and this was the king who wanted to kill him. The man who was seeking to kill him was feeding him involuntarily and unwittingly! Now that's fat–calf living. God took it from the table of the king and gave it to His prophet, Elijah.

All the things you are interested in and saving for "shall be added unto you" (Matthew 6:33) supernaturally. Remember, "we walk by faith, not by sight" (II Corinthians 5:7).

I leave you with one final admonition and faith challenge. **Prove God now** and see if He will not open the windows of Heaven and pour you out a blessing, until you do not have room to receive it (Malachi 3:10).

God is looking for people who want to be a blessing.

You won't have to *ask* for a blessing if you concentrate on *being* a blessing. Whatever you want to receive, spend time putting that out to others.

> ...For thine [God's] eyes are open upon all the ways of the sons of men: to give every one according to his ways, and according to the fruit of his doings.
>
> Jeremiah 32:19

# A Word from the Lord

God spoke to me sometime ago while I was in prayer for more understanding on this subject. He gave me a challenge to present to people when I minister. Here is what I heard in my spirit.

**Gerald, tell My people this:**
> Take $1,000 out of any investment that you presently have your money in and sow it to help reach Russia with Bibles. Wait six months for your return blessing to develop (increase on your investment). If you don't see an obvious development or change for the better in your life, which exceeds your present investment return, write to Gerald Davis and he will send the $1,000 back to you!

We sent enough money to Russia for over 100,000 Bibles on this challenge. Here is just one of the testimonies I've received from people who determined to do this to "prove God."

April 22, 1992

Dear Gerald Davis,

In November of 1991, my husband, David, quit his engineering job...in California, so we could return to Michigan where we were from and where our family was—"Our Heart's Desire."

Everyone said we were crazy to give up such a good job in a time of recession just to return home. We had some money to live on while David looked for a job, but we were close to the end when you came and preached about liberal giving. At offering time I asked David how much to make the check out to you for, and he said $1,000.00, which I did....

On March 30, 1992, we received a phone call for a job interview for an engineering job at almost the same pay David left [the previous company] at, and he started the job April 13, 1992. Everyone who hears of it is amazed. No one thought David would get such a good job in northern Michigan at this time of the year and at that salary. God is good, and liberal giving works, and we will continue to do so. Thank you, Gerald Davis!

David and Sharon

NOW RISE UP and CROSS OVER THE LINE! Prove God. Choose to enjoy Heaven's economy NOW!

"Peace be within thy walls, and prosperity within thy palaces" (Psalm 122:7).

# Study Notes

## Chapter 1
## Study Notes

**I.   The Father's Need**
Text: Matthew 7:11

A. The Nature of God

B. God's Desire Is to Give

C. God's Purpose for Creating Man
   1. To bless man
   2. To fulfill His need to give

D. The Devil Deceived Us
   1. We lost in every area of life

E. God's Remedy
   1. Jesus battled Satan and regained our position as joint-heirs with Him
      a. Luke 11:22

F. How Much Does God Want to Bless Us?
   1. Four illustrations

      a. The woman at the well
         1) John 4:1-42
      b. Mary and Martha
         1) Luke 10:38-42
      c. The two men on the road to Emmaus
         1) Luke 24:13-32
      d. The Prodigal Son
         1) Luke 15:11-32
            a) Where do you stand?

G. Summary
   1. The carnal nature versus the spiritual nature

**Notes**

# Chapter 2
# Study Notes

II. **Prosperity by Default**
Text: Deuteronomy 8:19-20, 9:3-6

A. Definitions of God's Grace and Mercy
   1. Your faith releases God's grace or favor to
      give you His gifts
      a. Salvation
      b. Healing
      c. Material supply
   2. God's mercy is unpredictable and unmerited

B. Prosperity Comes by Default (by God's Grace through
   Faith)
   1. You can lose your prosperity
   2. The Children of Israel received prosperity by
      default of the heathen nations
      a. Deuteronomy 9
   3. The Gentiles received salvation and prosperity by
      default of the Jews
      a. Romans 11:11-22
      b. Romans 4:3, 5, 13, 16, 20-25

C. Your New Promised Land Is Filled with Abundance
   1. God adds to and multiplies your life
      a. Deuteronomy 8:7-13
      b. Proverbs 10:22
   2. God prospers you
      a. To further His kingdom
         1) Deuteronomy 8:18
      b. Because He gets pleasure from giving good
         gifts to His children
         1) Psalm 37
         2) Luke 12:32
         3) Psalm 103:5
   3. Satan subtracts from and divides your life
      a. John 10:10

D. God Takes from the Ungodly and Gives to the Righteous
   1. Five witnesses (II Corinthians 13:1)
      a. Isaiah 43:1-4
      b. Proverbs 21:18
      c. Ecclesiastes 2:26
      d. Job 27:13, 16, 17
      e. Psalms 37:7, 9

   2. The wealth of the sinner is laid up for you
      a. He did it for me; He will do it for you
      b. Do not seek the wealth of others
         1) Seek God
      c. How can you possess *your* Promised Land?
         1) **Seek** God first
         2) **Obey** God's instructions
         3) **Believe** aggressively for your Promised Land
         4) **Talk** like you believe
         5) **Look** for it
         6) **Do** things to generate it
         7) **Obey** God's instructions for your life
         8) **Be generous** and liberal in your giving
            a) Proverbs 11:25

   E. Summary

**Notes**

# Chapter 3
# Study Notes

## III. The Prosperity of Fools
   Text: Proverbs 1:32

   A. The Prosperity of Fools Will Destroy Them
      1. Prosperity of money
         a. Warnings
            1) Deuteronomy 32:9-15

        2) Matthew 13:22
        3) Mark 10:23-26
        4) Proverbs 22:7
    b. Blessings
        1) Acts 20:35
        2) Matthew 6:33
        3) Deuteronomy 8:18
  2. Keep your priorities straight
    a. Do not fear riches
    b. Destroy the curse of poverty
    c. Avoid convenience for oneself
    d. Overcome the dangers and pitfalls

B. Summary

**Notes**

# Chapter 4
# Study Notes

## IV. What It Means to Be a Liberal Soul
Text: Proverbs 11:24-25

A. The Liberal Soul Shall Be Made Fat
  1. More than enough
    a. Being a liberal soul is not a deed you do, but something you are
    b. Law of Release
        1) Deuteronomy 15

2. Liberal versus non-liberal soul
   a. Comparisons between the liberal and non-liberal souls
   b. "The Key to Living Is Giving" (Poem)
3. Liberal soul mentality
   a. Think liberally in your heart
      1) Proverbs 23:7
   b. Deviseth liberal things
      1) Isaiah 32:8
   c. Scatter, yet increase
      1) Proverbs 11:24
   d. Illustration from personal experience
4. The prophet's challenge
   a. Are you committed to obeying God even in preference to losing money, if necessary?
   b. Can you trust God to restore your loss?
   c. **Obedience** is the issue
      1) Not money

B. Summary

# Notes

# Chapter 5
# Study Notes

## V. Giving with Receiving in Mind: Right or Wrong?
Text: Luke 6:38

A. Is It Right to Give with Receiving in Mind?
  1. Expect to receive
    a. Parable of the unjust steward
      1) Luke 16:1-9
      2) Invested in employer's debtors
    b. Adam versus Jesus
      1) Genesis 3
      2) Invested in God's debtors—people
  2. Sowing and reaping
    a. God sowed Jesus to receive man back
      1) John 3:16
      2) God gave with receiving in mind
    b. It is scriptural to give and receive
      1) Luke 6:38
  3. Two methods to obtain money
    a. Hoe Principle
      1) The world's method
    b. Shovel Principle
      1) God's method
    c. Look to God for a return

B. Summary

## Notes

# Chapter 6
# Study Notes

**VI. Windows in Heaven and a Cup Running Over (Personal Testimony)**
Text: Malachi 3:8-12

   A. You Cannot Contain All God's Blessings
      1. God's principle
         a. Luke 6:38
      2. Tithe and offering
         a. Malachi 3:8-12
      3. Knowledge of God's Word
         a. I Peter 5:8
      4. God can be trusted
      5. Illustrations
         a. Land
         b. Arabian horse
         c. Diesel engine

   B. Summary

# Notes

# Chapter 7
# Study Notes

## VII. Tares among the Good Seed
Text: Matthew 13:24-30

A. Three Measures of Meal (Matthew 13:33)
1. Spiritual
   a. John 10:10
2. Physical
   a. Matthew 14:36
   b. Matthew 12:15
   c. I Peter 2:24
3. Material
   a. Matthew 13:8
   b. III John 2

B. Tares among the Good Seed
1. Good News/Gospel
2. Bad news/tares
3. How to rightly divide the Word of Truth

C. Summary

## Notes

# Chapter 8
# Study Notes

**VIII. Six Hindrances to Receiving Your Harvest**
Text: Ecclesiastes 7:14

A. Consider Why You Are Not Experiencing Abundance after Sowing
   1. Woe versus blessing
      a. Consider "the wind that hinders sowing"
         1) Natural reasoning
      b. Consider "the clouds that hinder reaping"
         1) Thoughts and attitudes
   2. Weightier matters of the law (Matthew 23:23)
      a. Judgment
         1) Judge yourself
         2) Justify others
      b. Mercy
         1) Be merciful to others
      c. Faith
         1) Have faith for His promises
   3. Doing the right thing the wrong way
      a. Man's way seemeth right
      b. But there is a scriptural way
   4. Six principles to claim the promise of prosperity after you have tithed and given offerings
      a. Create the proper husband and wife relationship
      b. Maintain positive attitude and words
      c. Put God first
      d. Abstain from strife
      e. Know the difference between a vow and faith giving

f. Follow up on good ideas
5. Three mental virtues
   a. Wisdom
   b. Understanding
   c. Knowledge

B. Summary

**Notes**

# Chapter 9
# Study Notes

## IX. What It Means to Be Dried out to the Devil
Text: Luke 11:24

A. Three Desires of God for His Children (III John 2)
   1. Prosper (materially)
   2. Be in health (physically)
   3. Prosper in your soul (spiritually)

B. Three Desires of Satan (John 10:10b)
   1. Steal
   2. Kill
   3. Destroy

C. Satan's Devices
   1. A roaring lion
      a. I Peter 5:8

2. Self-condemnation
   a. Romans 8:1
3. An angel of light
   a. Galatians 1:8
4. As a bird
   a. Mark 4:3-4
5. Little foxes
   a. Song of Solomon 2:15

D. Summary

**Notes**

# Chapter 10
# Study Notes

X. **Due Season, Tough Times and Light Afflictions**
Text: II Corinthians 4:15-18

A. Due Season (Galatians 6:9)
   1. Type of seed
      a. Mushroom versus acorn seed
   2. Give "as unto the Lord"
   3. Soil of your heart
      a. Love
      b. Hope
      c. Faith

    4. Prepare yourself
      a. Set goals
      b. Make decisions about what to sow toward
      c. Cultivate your soil
      d. Abandon foolishness
    5. Security = faith in the integrity of God

B. Tough Times (II Corinthians 4:8-9)
    1. Bitter versus better
    2. Tough times work for you—not against you
      a. II Corinthians 4:17

C. Light Afflictions (II Corinthians 4:17)
    1. Light versus heavy
    2. Four anchors
      a. Love
      b. Faith
      c. Hope
      d. Praise

D. Summary

# Notes

# Chapter 11
# Study Notes

**XI. What to Do if Your Brook Dries Up!**
Text: I Kings 17:1-16

A. Don't Panic
   1. Jeremiah 33:3

B. Don't Let the Devil Put You under Condemnation
   1. John 14:1

C. Be Ready for Change
   1. I Kings 17:9

D. Be Ready to Make a Sacrificial Donation to Someone Else's Need
   1. God has two things in mind
      a. The need you have been praying about
      b. The need to which He has told you to give

E. Learn the Grace of Receiving
   1. I Kings 17:13

F. Summary

**Notes**

# Chapter 12
# Study Notes

## XII. The Secret to Obtaining Scriptural Wealth
Text: Matthew 6:19-20

A. The Secret to Wealth
   1. The power to get wealth
      a. Deuteronomy 8:18
   2. Samson's secret
      a. God's covenant
         1) Judges 13-16
         2) Isaiah 54:17
   3. Our secret
      a. Matthew 13:11
   4. Pursuit of knowledge and hidden treasures
      a. Proverbs 2:1-5

B. The Laws of Heaven
   1. Concerning finances
      a. Matthew 13:12
   2. The parable of the pounds
      a. Luke 19:12–26

C. High-Risk Investments Versus No-Risk Investments
   1. Treasures on earth versus treasures in Heaven
      a. Matthew 6:19-20

D. Summary

## Notes

# Chapter 13
# Study Notes

## XIII.  God's Plan for Old Age
Text: Psalm 92:12–15

A. God's Social Security Program
   1. How it works
      a. Philippians 4:15–19
   2. Our Treasurer—**Jesus**
      a. Hebrews 7:8
   3. High returns
      a. Luke 6:38
      b. Malachi 3:10

B. Blessings for Giving Tithes and Offerings
   1. "Windows–in–Heaven" blessing
      a. Malachi 3:10
   2. God rebukes the devourer for your sake
      a. Malachi 3:11
   3. God's promise for lending to Him
      a. Proverbs 19:17
      b. Proverbs 22:9
      c. Proverbs 28:27
      d. Proverbs 28:8

C. Be the Head and Not the Tail
   1. Lifestyle in abundance
      a. Deuteronomy 28:2-13
      b. Malachi 3:12
   2. Everything you are investing in and saving for "shall be added unto you" supernaturally

a. Matthew 6:33
3. Conclusion
   a. Jeremiah 32:19
   b. Psalm 122:7

D. Summary

E. A Word from the Lord

# Notes

# Special Information

To receive mail and ministry information from Gerald Davis, please write to OVERFLOWING CUP MINISTRIES at the address below.

We are sponsoring this book and others to be freely distributed in Russia. To share offerings with this ministry to help with our Missionary outreaches and book publications in Russia, please make checks payable to:

OVERFLOWING CUP MINISTRIES
P.O. Box 1286
New Caney, TX 77357
(281) 429-2891

Visit Gerald Davis Overflowing Cup Ministries online:

E-mail address:
gdavis@vonl.com

Web site address:
http://www.churches.com/gdm

Many people have shared about the effect these messages have had in their lives. If you have a story to tell—a testimonial from your life due to the teachings from this book—we would appreciate hearing from you. Any information you share may be used to help encourage others.

For more information about the soul-winning ministry of Gerald's son, Jerry Davis, or for a catalog and price list (for books, videos and audio tapes), please write to the address above.

# Price List

## Audio Cassettes
### Two–Tape Sets
But What About Jōb?.................................................................$14.00
How To Stop the Killing, Stealing and Destroying.......................$14.00
Victory Over Heart Trouble.......................................................$14.00

### Three–Tape Sets
The Liberal Soul.......................................................................$19.00
The Spirit of a Mountain Mover.................................................$19.00

### Four–Tape Sets
Developing Strong Faith............................................................$24.00
Holy Spirit...............................................................................$24.00
How To Generate Financial Blessing..........................................$24.00
Hundred Fold Living.................................................................$24.00
Know Your Enemy....................................................................$24.00
Most Requested Sermons..........................................................$24.00
Prosperity and Blessing............................................................$24.00
Sermons that Build Your Courage..............................................$24.00
Teaching on Faith....................................................................$24.00
Understanding for Overcomers..................................................$24.00

### Six–Tape Sets
How to Live in this Economy According to Heaven's Economy........$30.00
Walking in Success...................................................................$30.00

## Video
Five Things that Hinder Reaping After You've Sown Your Seed........$20.00
Giving With Receiving in Mind and Prosperity by Default.................$20.00
How to Invest Without Fear and Never Take a Loss.......................$20.00
The Liberal Soul.......................................................................$20.00
The Purpose of the Crown of Thorns..........................................$20.00

## Books
*15 Most Commonly Asked Questions on Tithing*..................................$ 2.50
*The Proper Attitude for Hundred-Fold Production*...............................$ 2.50
*The Importance of Keeping Up Your Joy Level*....................................$ 4.00
*Azusa Street Till Now* by Clara Davis.................................................$ 4.00
*But What About Jōb?*.......................................................................$ 4.00

(Please add 10% for shipping and allow 4-6 weeks for delivery.)
Mail to: Overflowing Cup Ministries
P.O. Box 1286 • New Caney, TX 77357

# Other Books by Gerald Davis

*15 Most Commonly Asked Questions About Tithing*
Foreword by Pastor John Osteen
     Houston, Texas


*The Proper Attitude For A One-Hundredfold Production:*
*Servants, Friends, Brethren*


*The Importance Of Keeping Up Your Joy Level*
Foreword by Evelyn Roberts
     Tulsa, Oklahoma


*But What About Jōb?*